WINE *HACK*

WINE *HACK*

WINE EDUCATION
THAT STARTS WITH YOUR MOUTH,
NOT WITH YOUR HEAD

JEFFREY SCHILLER

New York

WINE *HACK*
WINE EDUCATION THAT STARTS WITH YOUR MOUTH, NOT WITH YOUR HEAD

Published in New York, New York, by Morgan James Publishing. Morgan James and The Entrepreneurial Publisher are trademarks of Morgan James, LLC. www.MorganJamesPublishing.com

The Morgan James Speakers Group can bring authors to your live event. For more information or to book an event visit The Morgan James Speakers Group at www.TheMorganJamesSpeakersGroup.com.

A **free** eBook edition is available with the purchase of this print book.

CLEARLY PRINT YOUR NAME ABOVE IN UPPER CASE

Instructions to claim your free eBook edition:
1. Download the BitLit app for Android or iOS
2. Write your name in **UPPER CASE** on the line
3. Use the BitLit app to submit a photo
4. Download your eBook to any device

ISBN 978-1-63047-631-1 paperback
ISBN 978-1-63047-632-8 eBook
ISBN 978-1-63047-633-5 hardcover
Library of Congress Control Number: 2015939522

In an effort to support local communities and raise awareness and funds, Morgan James Publishing donates a percentage of all book sales for the life of each book to Habitat for Humanity Peninsula and Greater Williamsburg

Get involved today, visit
www.MorganJamesBuilds.com

Habitat
for Humanity®
Peninsula and
Greater Williamsburg
Building Partner

For my mom

CONTENTS

Prologue   *ix*

Chapter 1   El Corazón del Problema   1

Chapter 2   All You Need to Know about Wine   12

Chapter 3   Explaining Some Science Behind the Magic   39

Chapter 4   Finding God: Food and Wine Pairing   61

Chapter 5   Advanced Concepts   83

Chapter 6   Story Time   95

Epilogue   Be a BOSS   111

Acknowledgments   *120*

About the Author   *123*

Further Resources   *125*

PROLOGUE

It's not your fault, Will . . . Listen to me, son. It's not your fault.
—Good Will Hunting

Have you ever read a wine description in a newspaper review or a food and wine magazine and immediately hated the author? "Aromas of cumquat, Florence fennel, and dragon fruit dance in the glass with layers of cassis, veal stock, and dried sage on the palate, finishing long and velvety." Thanks, Dickens, but will I actually like this wine as much as you enjoyed writing that little poem? Am I drinking a fruit salad or a vegetable-pie smoothie? Would you describe Coca-

Cola like that? How about chicken noodle soup? What is so different about wine?

Wine is ultimately just a beverage, and while it affords this author regular romance, profound life lessons, intriguing histories of diverse cultures, a career, great friendships, and a life rich with gustatory ecstasy, I would have to consider it the world's third best beverage. Coffee delivers a far more important drug than alcohol, and then there's whisky: sometimes you don't need romance; you just need a drink.

In short, wine can be overblown. The reasons for this? In many cases, inequality of information allows those with more information to confuse those who don't have much information, and regularly to the advantage of those with it. My Wall Street friends can attest to how well this works. In some cases, marketers rely on puffery when the true character or the quality of a wine are actually wanting. For the defensible few, it's because there's genuine passion, artistry, and a life's pursuit in every bottle. The immeasurable blood, sweat, tears, bad weather, vineyard pests, plant diseases, early mornings, late nights, barrel-rolling, wine-racking, tank-cleaning, and marathon tastings that go into *one* vintage of *one* wine indeed merit faithful worship of the art of winemaking. Or, as explained more succinctly by many winemakers, it takes a lot of good beer to make good wine. Through this lens, wine is deservedly complex.

For fledgling students of wine, the challenges of understanding wine are significant. First, illogically, the major differences across wines are subtle. Deciphering subtlety takes practice. It also isn't easy to teach or explain a sensory experience. How can any expert argue with what a person *says* they taste? Regardless, and not coincidentally, perhaps as many as 90 percent of wine drinkers can't articulate what they like, much less why. But it's not their fault. "Don't f*** with me; not you, Sean, not you!" It's not your fault. Nobody teaches the wine-drinking public a consistent language to articulate what they are tasting or what they like. Journalists, educators, retailers, and waitstaff can all fail you, and regularly do.

For those who don't have the inclination to read up on the Chardonnay clones of Burgundy, nor the means or access to barrel-taste upcoming Bordeaux releases, nor the time to track weather patterns over a favorite winemaking region, the experience remains convoluted and intimidating—or, as my sometimes feisty mother would say, "frustrating as hell." For those wine drinkers and for my mother, I have the solution. Wine doesn't need to be so difficult.

With this book, I want to take the undeserved elitism out of wine drinking and make it accessible to everyone. I will build your wine vocabulary, and I will give you the Rosetta stone that unlocks the simple attributes that all those elitist words represent. We will rob the wine douchetocracy of its power with elementary notions that you will be able to articulate to the people who sell you wine. It is my goal to make you as comfortable choosing between a Sancerre and a Muscadet as you are choosing between an iced tea and iced latte.

How can I possibly make all of these promises? If it's been made so complex by so many, what possible reason can I offer to explain how I—the idiot who used double-spacing and manipulated fonts and margins to stretch term papers to the required ten pages, and the same prodigy who inserted the Gettysburg Address into a research paper because he couldn't find enough to say about Abraham Lincoln—can create a marked change in people's ability to learn about wine via a book? In a word, the answer is: food. You already know what foods you like and why. We can learn about and discuss wine with this common foundation that everyone understands and, more importantly, experiences. We'll draw parallels from food to inform your understanding of wine.

Plus, know that moments of success happen every day. There are so many outstanding sommeliers and restaurant owners across the country who are knowledgeable and agile in attending to their customers; they're people who operate in a very competitive restaurant environment and don't make money if you're not delighted. I assure you that they start with the same deductive approach that permeates this book:

identifying and then articulating the profiles of the wines you like. Remember this notion of a wine profile; we'll come back to this. Tell a sommelier (or somm for short) what you like, or normally drink, and they'll find something similar for the amount of money you're willing to shell out. This is how people meet wines they like every day.

So you could argue that, with this book, I have not labored through research and analysis to discover a groundbreaking master key that unlocks all of the mysteries of wine. You could argue that I have, in fact, simply consolidated the proven practices and known truths of those who are best in the business at helping people find the wines they like. You could say that this book isn't novel in approach or original in its content. And you'd be right.

But I believe this is the first book on wine education that starts with your mouth, not your head. This comes naturally to me, of course, always talking before I think. For you, it means you get a personal, unassailable experience to validate what you actually taste in a glass, rather than taking my word for it. I hope you will use the shopping list in the back of this book so that you can taste what I'm teaching. #TeachYoMouth moments are littered throughout the book to deliver that unassailable tasting experience, guaranteeing you learn the language of wine. Try it at home by yourself, section by section, or invite friends over and make a night of it.

I wouldn't be doing my job if I didn't make an attempt to explain why these differences exist. To fully understand anything, we must distill the symptoms down to the disease. With wine, it's tracing the stylistic differences back to their root causes: climate, soil, winemaking decisions, tiny miracles. This "why" isn't essential for you to build your wine language skills, but for the curious, these root causes will cement in your mind the readily apparent differences in wine, and all of this is readable in a medium-length flight. What, were you going to watch reruns of *How I Met Your Mother* or season two of *True Blood*? (Seriously, Delta, please step it up.)

Okay, don't tell my publisher, but truth be told, you only need to read chapter 2. If your time is short or your attention span millennial, start there and—you won't hurt my feelings—end there. Because after that chapter, you will be able to tell any sommelier, wine shop attendant, and your mother exactly what you like and don't like, and why. This newfound fluency in wine will allow you to explore with more success and enjoyment. I'm excited for you; I hope you are excited too.

CHAPTER 1

EL CORAZÓN DEL PROBLEMA

Model: *I could listen to you talk about mail all day.*
Newman: *Anything you wish . . . I'll tell you a little secret about zip codes: they're meaningless.*
                    —*Seinfeld*, 1997

I was studying for an MBA when I first became a willing and eager student of wine. Monetary policy and advanced regression were distilled down into chapters and classes and tests. It was all learnable with an investment of time. Imagine my frustration, perhaps much like yours as a student of wine, when after a year of reading books, I still didn't understand what I was tasting. I spent my days tackling the complexities of money supply, antitrust law, and balance sheets. Surely somewhere in the wine world someone had stumbled upon a simplifying theory, framework, or even cheap tricks to teach you this beverage. Bordeaux, Barolo, Pinot Noir, Pinot Gris, American Oak, Brix, acidity—how do I understand everything from the rigid technicalities to the flowery poetry these experts espouse in the vast expanse of wine education?

Every book I found started with information to fill your head. Nobody started with the beverage in your mouth. Most of the educational resources start with lists of the first growths of Bordeaux and varietal descriptions, maps of winegrowing regions, and technical descriptions of the fermentation process—a dog's breakfast. They give you no order, reasoning, or explanation of what it means in regard to the wine you taste. It's not to say the information that they offer isn't fantastic. Don't think for a second that I didn't geek out learning that Rioja's ascension to the winemaking world started when a tiny bug almost wiped out all of Bordeaux's vines in the late 1800s, or that I don't appreciate how archaic Napoleonic inheritance laws still influence the way the great wines of Burgundy are made to this day. All of that book learning is great, but it has an Achilles leg.

Learning wine is very much like learning a foreign language. I was fluent in Spanish after studying throughout high school and college, living nonconsecutive years in Madrid and Buenos Aires, and having a very demanding Nicaraguan girlfriend. With a foreign language, you first have to learn the vocabulary, learning to express yourself without regard for grammar or rules. Then it takes practice to learn the grammar and rules for all situations. Wine is no different in that sense; you have to first learn a vocabulary to express what you're tasting. Then you need lots of practice, learning to apply that vocabulary to all the wines that come your way. Without the vocabulary, however, conversation is difficult. I've pursued a two-year, $10,000 educational program with the Wine & Spirits Educational Trust, which alone has brought me hundreds of hours of tasting. Professionally, I've probably spent over 2,000 hours tasting wine to become fluent. But nobody in the wine world ever really starts their education with "*Dónde está la biblioteca?*" and "*Cómo estás?"* They hand you a copy of *Don Quixote* in Spanish and assume you already have the vocabulary.

To their credit, the major trade publications—such as *The Wine Advocate*, *Wine Enthusiast Magazine*, *Food & Wine*, and *Wine Spectator*—have done a lot of heavy lifting to get people to where they are today. The 100-point score systems are helpful, as are their lists of recommendations and pairings in monthly issues. But because the number of wines is so great and the distribution of wine so fragmented, people are regularly challenged when wines from a magazine's list of, say, the best summer Chardonnays, aren't available at the restaurant or wine shop of their choice. It's like having a cheat sheet, but to a different test.

Joel McHale, Wine Guru

I get frustrated when reading tasting notes and scores in the major wine publications. These reviews provide little insight into the wine the writers are supposedly sharing with us. Here are two reviews of two different wines from the same issue of one publication. Guess which one was rated 93 points and which one 87 points?

Shows juicy energy, with savory, pomegranate, red currant, iron, and singed anise notes all woven together and backed by a long, iron-tinged finish that lets the sanguine hint echo.

Crisp, focused flavors of black cherry and fresh herbs mingle with light smoke and licorice notes in this lively red. Features a racy energy, with snappy tannins and fresh acidity.

If you were able to choke down the vomit, refrain from scratching out your eyes, and power through the written masturbation of "sanguine hint echo," you probably noticed that these wine descriptions, despite significant differences in score, suggest no other major difference in quality or style. One received 87 points, meaning "very good: a wine with special qualities," and one received 93 points, meaning "outstanding: a wine of superior quality and style." While the explanation of these scores provides some CYA, a 6-point gap on a 100-point scale, when they rarely publish anything about wines that rate below 80, seems material. Were you able to guess which was which?

More importantly, how do these two comparable reviews help you decide which wine to buy? These notes have become the established benchmarks for talking about wine, but they fail to communicate anything worthwhile to the reader, and they definitely don't help you predict whether or not you will like the wine. I imagine many of you have read a spectacularly delicious description of a wine, only to push away the glass with disappointment. Wine lists, handwritten notes posted to the shelves of wine shops, descriptions on winery websites, articles in the newspaper—we in the industry seem content peddling flowery prose as expert advice.

A fair counterargument to my criticizing these publications would be that such reviews are made for those who work in the business, not the wine-drinking public. Fair point, this is mostly true. But guess what? Nobody in the industry uses, much less reads, tasting note nonsense. When working with winemakers, you would never hear me rattle off a list of flavors to communicate the character or quality of a wine. It might be a component of the discussion, but typically we would just note how complex it was, and then talk about other things entirely to find a common understanding of a wine. What are those other things? Keep reading.

Unfortunately, this short-form poetry is the lexicon that inevitably leaks out to laypeople. Those new to the wine industry think this is what wine is about and these geeks proliferate the problem when they interact with everyday humans who only speak Earth languages. On their own, flavor descriptions are like zip codes: meaningless. Veterans of the wine trade know that an esoteric description of flavors will never sum up the experience of a wine.

I read a great interview with comedian Joel McHale in the July 2014 issue of *Food & Wine*, talking about his life before he blew up on the national stage: "I worked at a wine store in LA when I first moved there. When it got busy, I had to sell the wine even though I didn't really know about it. I would just say, 'dark fruits, blackberries, and cigars.'"

Why wouldn't he? Tell people what they want to hear, and move on.

The alternative, of course, is to establish a shared language that allows people to articulate what they like and interact with wine sellers—a common lens through which every wine is judged, a lens that doesn't bend as each wine is examined, and that showcases the material differences among wines.

Happy Places

Why bother with this? First, I'm annoyed with these people in my industry who make wine unnecessarily difficult, if you can't already tell.

Second, and this is at the heart of this book, there's so much more enjoyment for everyday drinkers to unlock from this extraordinary beverage. Just as the difference between well-done and medium-rare affects your satisfaction with a steak, the ratio of olive oil to vinegar changes your opinion of a salad, and the level of complexity of flavors in your pad Thai makes or breaks your Thai dinner, the texture, balance, and complexity of a wine inevitably dictate your experience with it. I want more people to understand and appreciate these factors and ultimately adore all of wine as much as I do.

Third, because wine is almost always accompanied by food, I want to make sure you know some simple rules that will help you pair wine with food and keep you from faulting a perfectly good wine for the effect of some overwhelming cuisine. I will free you from the many silly myths of food and wine pairing. A couple basic principles you already know intuitively just need to be repackaged. You probably already know that there are only five tastes the human mouth can sense (sweet, sour, salty, bitter, and savory).[1] With this book, I promise that you can forge an understanding of how they interact with wine, preventing you from unfairly punishing the lovely wine you are drinking. Call it the Hippocratic Oath of Wine Pairing: first, do no harm. Wine will rarely corrupt the meal you are having, because more of those five tastes, if not all five, are likely at work in your dinner, whereas your wine might only have three, likely only two, of those tastes in the glass. In short, food can overpower the wine and corrupt the experience. After simply mastering "do no harm" with easy-to-remember rules, you are free to explore and enjoy, because the possibilities are truly infinite.

But first, we will put to pasture the standard, inadequate tasting note and its hackneyed attempts to objectively communicate the qualities of a wine. We will build a new, simpler vocabulary that will allow you to explore the great wine regions of the world and the great stylistic differences of different winemakers. You will soon fearlessly navigate to what

---

1 American and Japanese scientists now claim to have isolated a sixth taste, but they can't agree exactly on what it is.

you truly enjoy, and create a construct to appreciate how your tastes and preferences evolve over time.

Before we get started, I have two disclaimers, one of which relates back to why learning wine is ultimately a worthwhile, almost religious endeavor. First, the many dynamics that create wine make a perfect understanding impossible. Italy alone has over 3,000 native grape varieties. Weather swings from vintage to vintage can make the very same wine outstanding in one year and mediocre in the next. A winemaker might leave a winery, an owner might decide to cut costs, or an importer might decide to stop importing certain wines, all of which means that your opportunity to experience consistency with the wines you love is fleeting. Consistency would make learning wine easier, but clearly, the cards are stacked against us.

Ever watch the movie *Somm*? It's a documentary about a small group of smart people studying for the hardest wine exam on the planet, the exam that makes you a master sommelier, of which there are just over 200 total in the world. In the movie, after the tasting portion of the exam, the best of the best couldn't agree on what the very first wine was in the blind tasting, with just about everyone citing a different answer: Pinot Grigio, Chenin Blanc, Riesling, Alvariño, and Sauvignon Blanc. Clearly, I'm not knocking these guys; blind-tasting esoteric wines is super-difficult, and they admit as much. However, it should illustrate to you at the outset, that it is quite literally impossible to know it all. Even the most knowledgeable sommeliers can't know everything.

That said, it doesn't mean you need to give up nor should you even be intimidated. You don't have to learn every fact about every wine ever produced; you can learn principles over facts and stylistic commonalities over labels and vintages. You don't have to know the perfect technique for squats or how many grams of sugar are in a beet to know how to live a healthy life. Like I said, learning about wine is like learning a foreign language, and while some people are lucky enough to grow up in bilingual homes (e.g., people who grow up in Napa or in a winemaking family), and some are naturally gifted at processing what they hear (e.g., people with measurably more taste buds on their tongue, "supertasters," of which my mother is one, I believe), the rest of us will need practice to learn this foreign language.

So don't cower in the face of this impossible complexity; embrace it and enjoy it. #TeachYoMouth the vocabulary. Besides, what is more fun than learning by drinking? I wish my college had offered that class. A bonus to mastering this vocabulary, for all the foodies out there, is the upgrade in your vocabulary for objectively measuring a restaurant or chef's cuisine. Complexity, balance, and texture are not just for wine; they are objective observations of food, too.

My second disclaimer is this: There's one thing, and it's really the only thing, that anyone can tell you when learning to understand and appreciate wine. Wine is highly personal, like any worthwhile experience. You ultimately decide whether you prefer the MOMA or the Met, Paris or London, Captain Kirk or Captain Picard, or Korean BBQ or Texas brisket. Never let anyone rob you of this personal interpretation of an artisanal, historic, decadent experience like wine. If you like Moscato for $6 a bottle, dammit, drink $6 Moscato and tell everyone else they are suckers for overpaying. Go ahead and try to give me crap for enjoying the delicious $3 carnitas tacos from a Napa taco truck, the $3.50 *Bahn mi* sandwich from the Saigon Sandwich Shop in San Francisco, the $1.35 Skyline cheese coney in Cincinnati, the $2 beignets from Café du Monde in New Orleans, the $2.19 fried chicken breakfast biscuit from Chick-fil-A, or any slice of pizza in New York City. These are my happy places. If Yellow Tail Moscato is your happy place, then show off your kangaroo lower back tattoo proudly.

Finally, and I swear I'm not stalling, there's one word that needs to soak in before we get started. Only one word: taste. Taste often, taste more, and taste with those who know more than you. Just as with Spanish, you'll get better the more you practice. The most fun you can have is putting two different glasses of wine side by side and simply observing the differences, swirling, smelling, and tasting, judging what you personally like better and finding the words to say why. We'll do this a lot in chapter 2 and it's essential to learning wine. Let's begin.

CHAPTER 2

ALL YOU NEED TO
KNOW ABOUT WINE

'Cause it's just another day in the life of the goddamn boss.
—Rick Ross

While you can't swipe left or "like" any part of this book, it is meant to be interactive. You can't simply read your way to wine knowledge; you have to taste your way there. So I'd ask that you not only read this book, but that you use it as your own personal tasting instructor. You'll need supplies for this safari. Rip out the Shopping List from the back of the book, pick up the suggested groceries and wines, and taste along as you read to truly *digest* the distinctions that each of the wines will express. My first pun! Drink! New rule: every time you read a pun, you have to take a sip of wine.

Truth be told, this book might make a far better app. But it costs like $100,000 to create a decent iPhone app, so we'll start with a book!

Before we begin tasting, I want to prepare your ears and eyes for some elitist words that might have intimidated you in the past. I'm going to use some of these words throughout the book—words like "structure" and "length." Don't be scared of them; I will teach you their meaning and they will lose their elitist power. Follow me through these pages and you will find more wines that you like and enjoy wine more frequently.

Be a BOSS

Welcome to the acronym that will help you conquer wine: BOSS. Yes, acronyms are lazy. And that's why they're perfect for my fellow Americans! I don't mean that as an insult. We all dedicate our time to things that are important—family, school, work, Candy Crush. We don't all have the luxury of spending 2,000 hours tasting wines to achieve proficiency. That is 100 percent of the reason why Robert Parker's

100-point score system works for wine collectors. And that is the reason we're using an acronym. My promise is to make this simple.

BOSS stands for body, oak, sweet, sour. All wines can be described by these four simple traits. Think of them as four sliding scales, like you might see on a sound system tuner. The adjustment up or down of the treble or bass creates a different experience for your ears. The adjustment of these BOSS traits creates different experiences in your mouth. Dialing up or down the body of a wine (from light-bodied to full-bodied), the oak flavor (from no oak at all to lots of oak), the sweetness (from totally dry to super-sweet), and the sourness (from high-acid or sourness to low-acid or not sour at all) is what creates the differences in wines.

Have you seen those sound systems that pre-populate the treble and bass settings based on the music you want to hear? Select "country" to enjoy Hank Williams, or "R&B" for Mary J. Blige's hits. Similarly, the BOSS "setting" of a wine will give you distinct wine experiences. In fact, in certain parts of the world, winemakers are legally required to produce to a specific style and you can generally count on certain regions to be consistent in how much body, oak, sweet, and sour you will find in the wine. Why? We shall discuss this in chapter 3. And oh, by the way, just as some days you need Dr. Dre's

The Chronic in your life, and other days you want to rock out to the Black Keys, some days you may want to adjust your mouth tuner to a big-bodied, high-tannin, low-acid Napa Valley Cabernet, instead of a delicate, floral, light-bodied, high-acid Sancerre. They are different experiences, but by no means better or worse. Just different.

Let's take each of these four BOSS components one by one and first explain them simply with words. Then, as promised, we'll taste everyday food or drink you're already familiar with to illustrate how the BOSS tuner may be dialed up or down. Finally, we will taste wines with fundamentally opposite BOSS profiles to drive home an intuitive understanding of each of the four BOSS traits.

It's one thing to read an idea and appreciate its *truthiness*; it's another entirely to faithfully agree with a statement because you've had the same experience. The latter is my hope. To serve that end, each of the #TeachYoMouth moments in this book is your opportunity to truly understand wine. If you haven't yet, snap a picture of or remove the Shopping List in the back of this book so that you can grab the essentials next time you're in a grocery store or wine shop.

Once you have mastered these four components, we'll put them all together in a nice little package for you to deliver to the snootiest wine snob, waiter, or wine shop dick. You'll officially be a BOSS.

If you're like me, you need to see it to learn it. So as we start, for the visual learners, picture your own personal wine tuner using a wine very close to my heart:

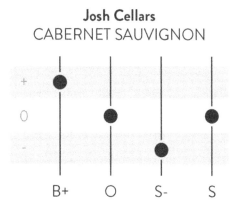

By book's end, we will have plotted out a variety of wines on this tuner. My hope is that you will come to identify the profiles of the wines you like and find a newfound freedom and confidence in exploring wines, navigating to what you like, understanding what you don't, and ultimately setting yourself up to enjoy wine for the rest of your life without fear of intimidation.

Body

Body is the only BOSS element that isn't actually a taste, making it slightly more difficult to intuitively understand than the rest. Body describes the weight of the wine in your mouth and the degree to which it consumes your entire mouth. The classic industry trick for understanding body involves, of all things, milk. Pour a glass of skim milk and a glass of whole milk and try them sequentially, paying close attention to the differences. What do you notice? The weight is different: whole milk just feels heavier. If your tongue were a scale, you would feel it buckle under the pressure of the heavier whole milk. It also expands beyond a narrow channel within your mouth and occupies more space as it passes over your tongue and works back to your throat. That simple notion of body can explain a lot of what you like in a wine.

For white wine drinkers, if you prefer the standard, run-of-the-mill Italian Pinot Grigio, rather than an oaky Napa Valley Chardonnay, you likely prefer light-bodied wines. For red wine drinkers, if you prefer a Burgundian Pinot Noir over an Argentine Malbec or an Australian Shiraz, you too enjoy a light-bodied wine. If you like a Burgundian Pinot Noir, you are likely to enjoy the delightful light-bodied wines of Italy's Nero D'Avola or Austria's Zweigelt. You don't *have* to like these alternatives, but they occupy a similar category that can be simply articulated as "light-bodied." Alternatively, those devotees of full-bodied wines, say monster wines like Penfolds Shiraz, Ridge Zinfandel, and Meiomi Pinot Noir, you are loving full-bodied wines. That's not to say that you have to like either light- or full-bodied wines only, nor does it mean that you have to like all the other wines that are light-bodied because you like one light-bodied wine. It's the same thing as connecting your love of One Direction and NSYNC, Talib Kweli and Common, or Elton John and Billy Joel; they are simply like genres. Price and quality ultimately play a role in what you might like, too, so if you only drink $100 Pinot Noir from the Côte de Nuits, a similarly light-bodied $15 Zweigelt might leave you disappointed. That's no different than your 99-cent cheeseburger from Wendy's being less satisfying as one from your local steakhouse. Like genres don't equate to equal quality, but they will help you narrow the playing field when seeking out wines you like.

I personally adore both Penfolds Grange, a full-bodied Shiraz ($600 per bottle), and Villa Pozzi Nero D'Avola ($10 per bottle), for the same reason I love (secretly, alone in my car) "We Are Never Ever Getting Back Together" by Taylor Swift and (proudly, windows down, looking like an idiot) "Hit 'Em Up," Tupac Shakur's nastiest trash-talking diss track. And the same reason I will eat $100-per-pound *pata negra jamón ibérico* for dinner and later that night have McDonald's deliver cheeseburgers to my apartment after too much whisky. They are different. I would argue that most days these things are neither better nor worse, just different. And yes, God bless New York City, McDonald's delivers. Let's get the lead out, Shake Shack.

Different occasions, different moods, different appetites, different crowds. I was recently chatting up a couple of nice people at a Miami airport bar, and they both forced me to pick my favorite New York City pizza. Why do we do this to ourselves? Why are we so intent on picking one at the expense of all the others? I told them I love multiple pizza places for multiple reasons. It's the same with wine; there is *so much* good wine on this planet. So many extraordinary people and families labor for money or love or both or neither to create wonderful wines. They can all be cherished. Most deservedly so.

Keep in mind that there are other differences in these wines that I've just lumped together. We still have to explore the other three components: oak, sweet, and sour. And there are a great many other differences, such as winemaker decisions and vineyard conditions, that may keep you from enjoying wines of the same genre. Your individual preferences for the other complexities in wine besides body have the right to trump any differences we taste in this one BOSS component. But to drive home the "B" in BOSS, these wines can be described as similar or different by their level of body.

Now let's embark on the first of several opportunities to #TeachYoMouth. Remember that the purpose of these tasting exercises isn't necessarily to give you examples of wines you will enjoy. Its purpose is to explain a BOSS component by showcasing the stylistic differences of two wines with opposite settings on the BOSS tuner. We'll start by illustrating the range of the "B" in BOSS. Now, if you like what you're drinking, bottoms up! The book isn't going anywhere; carve up some cheese and charcuterie and get your drink on—you've earned it. Just plan to #LearnByDrinking next weekend.

#TeachYoMouth Moment: Body

Non-wine example: There is no simpler way to illustrate the quality of body in a wine than the milk test. If you didn't try this already when I referenced it earlier, do it now. Drink a glass of whole milk after a glass of skim milk. How much fuller, rounder, and most importantly, heavier is the whole milk? Notice the whole milk weighing down your tongue, applying pressure against the entirety of your mouth. The skim milk, by contrast, is suddenly thin, watered-down, and hollow.

You've just learned how the "B" in BOSS can range from light-bodied to full-bodied. Now let's apply it to wine.

Wine example: Try the following two white wines side by side. Go back and forth between the two and see if you can validate the following profile. Important note: body isn't something you taste. It isn't a flavor; it isn't something your taste buds will spot. It is an attribute of density. Look for the weight difference only, just like you did in the milk test. You will notice other differences, which we'll eventually get to, but first just notice the difference in body and weight in your mouth.

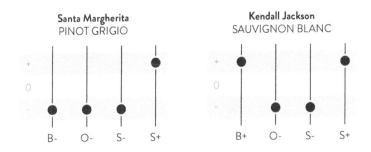

Now try the following two red wines side by side. Go back and forth between the two and see if you can pull out these profile differences in the following wines:

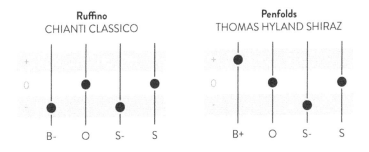

It's okay if you didn't notice the differences exactly as I've described them in your first taste test. In fact, as you taste your way along the wine-learning curve, you might not always experience the differences as clearly as I list them in each section. Don't give up. It will take practice. Keep trying. I promise you can #TeachYoMouth. How can I make that promise? When I started learning wine, the only difference I could spot between two different wines was the color. Many of the people listed in the acknowledgements of this book can attest to that fact. If I learned it, so can you.

While you practice, I'll offer you a shortcut, a wine version of "up-up-down-down-left-right-left-right-B-A-B-A-Select-Start" to suggest what sort of body the wine has. Check the label for alcohol. The answer is printed right there on the label. While not a perfect measure in isolation, it gives you a pretty good idea of how big-bodied your wine is, as alcohol is one of the things that contributes to body. We'll cover this in more detail in chapter 3, but for now know that wines under 13.0 percent I would consider Tara Reid, 13.0–14.5 percent are Jennifer Connelly from the late 1990s, and anything over 14.5 percent is Kim Kardashian.

For those of you who have successfully seen the distinction in your very first tasting, isn't this fun? You just had four tastes of wine and have compartmentalized the differences in nice, neat little charts. By the time you have read another 16 pages, you will have mastered all four factors that you'll need to chat wine with anyone. If you're a lightweight, you might also be a little tipsy. Plan for an Uber.

Oak

If you drink tea, the impression of oak can be easily explained. When you leave the tea bag in hot water for too long, what happens to the tea? Doesn't it get supremely bitter? There is also an astringent, desiccating sensation around your lips and gums. Wine aged in oak can leave that same bitter taste and astringency as tea. There is no coincidence that both tea and oak barrels come from plants. Tannin is the common chemical compound in plants that protects them from disease and rot. Tannin is what creates the desiccation. Tannin makes it into your wine not only from the oak barrels in which it was aged, but also from the skins, seeds, and stems of the grapes. More on this later.

Why are we talking about oak and why is this your problem? Most importantly, oak is the preferred wood for aging your wine. While the choice of oak might seem arbitrary, know that wine is mostly the result of centuries of trial and error, and making the best of what was available. God bless the monks. The Catholic Church was awful in a lot of ways for most of its career, but these clever, thirsty hermits were the best at consolidating and reapplying the best practices of wine. (Beer too. Thank you, Trappists.) After years of trial and error by monks and other early winemakers, oak eventually became the wood barrel of choice, being excellent at contributing pleasant flavors like oak, vanilla, and baking spices like cinnamon, and adding tannin that creates the dryness, structure, and longevity that people seek.

Did you see what I did there? I just nonchalantly snuck in two beefy concepts, *structure* and *longevity*. We'll come back to those in chapter 5. For now, let's just appreciate that oak adds this bitter, drying sensation and note that it has other benefits.

As I mentioned, the source of this bitterness is the naturally occurring tannin in grape seeds and skins or the oak barrels stripped from the French, American, or Hungarian forests. Make no mistake; it has the same effect in your mouth as broccoli or black coffee. If you take milk and sugar in your coffee, you are trying to temper the bitter.

For those who crave "smooth" red wines like Apothic Red, Ménage à Trois, or Meiomi, you are not likely to be a fan of tannin and oak, preferring a low-tannin wine. For those of you who enjoy Bordeaux, Barolo, or the oaky Napa Valley Chardonnay, you are a fan of that bitterness and tannin. You want some "O" in your BOSS.

#TeachYoMouth Moment: Oak

Non-wine example: Drink black coffee and then coffee with milk. My guess is that you can imagine this without actually tasting them, but there's more wine to drink, so a little coffee might be good for you. You can also imagine boiled broccoli and a boiled potato. There is no bitterness in that potato, but how bitter is that broccoli? Bitter tends to make itself known at the end of the tasting experience. Try a cup of tea with the tea bag soaked for two minutes and another cup soaked for five minutes. Notice that desiccation and intense drying from the five-minute soaked tea. You will notice that very same effect in wines with and without extended oak aging.

Wine example: Now let's apply this to wine, using low-oak Sauvignon Blanc from Kendall Jackson and high-oak Kendall Jackson Chardonnay.

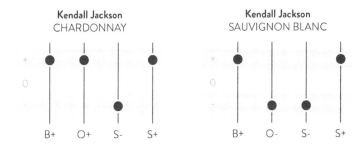

As you taste these wines, be on the lookout for the classic signatures of oak: vanilla and dill flavors, and of course, duh, the flavor of oak. Also, notice the bitterness. Oak makes the wine bitter, like the sensation you get from chewing on a toothpick, or when you've finished a Popsicle but have nowhere to throw the stick so you chew on it. The bitterness of oak will play an integral part in food and wine pairing later, so take stock now of this oak influence. Your preference for or against oak will also help you zero in on wines you like.

If you're wondering why I'm not offering up a red wine version, it's mainly because so few red wines are made without oak. It's easy to find a wine with this profile:

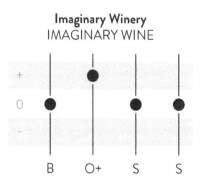

But it's quite difficult to show you this one:

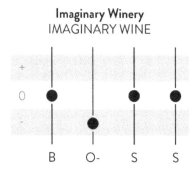

There are so few widely distributed red wines without oak that I don't feel like I'm cheating you on this #TeachYoMouth moment. Beaujolais Nouveau is one, but, unfortunately, it's only available for a few months of the year.

For those of you unfamiliar with Beaujolais Nouveau, buckle up. This is one of the most distinct wine creatures on the planet and easily one of its most pleasant table wines, French or otherwise. It was hot in the 1980s. Skinny pants and aviators came back, but, sadly, this beautiful winemaking tradition has not, and I don't understand why. Nouveau is not made through traditional winemaking techniques, but instead through a rare fermentation process known as carbonic maceration. Big words aside, it is the very first wine released every vintage, arriving the third Thursday in November. Let me repeat this: it is the *first* wine of every vintage. It was quite literally a holiday in England back in the day. In Japan, it remains an over-the-top celebration every year, where the most eccentric revelers enjoy hot baths in the newly released wine. Where are you at, America? In a country that has made NFL Sundays more important than Sunday dinner, a country whose adults have stolen Halloween from the children so they can dress up and party like children, and a country that now celebrates Cinco de Mayo not in honor of Mexican independence but because the winter sucked and nobody hates Coronas, how do we *not* celebrate the first wine of every vintage? If nothing else, it's a reason to start drinking wine around midnight on a Wednesday. I ask my fellow New Yorkers, why are we not on board?

In any case, it remains one of the few unoaked red wines. Look for it in November.

Sweet

Sweetness should be the most straightforward concept, but its misuse in describing wine is probably the greatest. Sweetness only comes from sugar. If wine is sweet, generally speaking, sugar is either added (in a low-cost wine) or prevented from fermenting (in an expensive wine), the latter being the source of the term *residual sugar*. The name comes from classic winemaking tradition and it's what's left over after fermentation, which we'll discuss in the science-y chapter, chapter 3. In more modern, low-cost approaches to making wine, sugar was likely added, but we still call it residual sugar. I promise we'll explore how all that happens in chapter 3. For now, know that residual sugar affects the experience, and in more ways that you would expect.

First and foremost, residual sugar in a wine will give you the obvious dessert-like experience that candy, ice cream, and fruit will. Sometimes a wine will be really fruity in its flavors, and people will call this sweet. Sometimes people will taste highly acidic or sour wines and call them sweet. These people are incorrect. Sweetness in wine is only about the measurable sugar.

Lesser known is the fact that sweetness also adds weight or body ("B") and soft texture. More specifically, sweetness makes the hard edges of oak and tannin softer, no different than when you put sugar in your coffee. In fact, winemakers will often deliberately dial up the residual sugar in a wine to create a smoother, rounder, softer wine. This doesn't necessarily make the wine sweet; it would still be perceived as dry, but the slight amount of residual sugar creates a big textural change. That sweetness can dull the astringency of tannin and can temper a high-acid wine.

Residual sugar in a wine can also be like the gooey, melted cheese on bad pizza. Lots of cheese can forgive the sins of crappy crust or bland sauce. Similarly, sweetness can cover up the sins from the vineyard and shortcomings of low-quality grapes. But it can also take a great wine and make it that much more satisfying, like gooey, fresh mozzarella on great pizza. There are some in the industry who might be angry about wineries adding sugar, but I don't see any reasons to hate on wines with higher residual sugar—do you want to enjoy wine, or not? My guess is that most of you have enjoyed a wine with higher residual sugar and didn't know it. Oh wait, unless those elitists at your wine shop or restaurant tell you that it's a problem. Don't listen to these knuckleheads; listen only to your mouth.

A great many wines in the marketplace have seen remarkable success by actually pushing beyond the bounds of what dry wines are. Meiomi, Apothic Red, and Ménage à Trois are all wines that have had extraordinary commercial success, and most wine industry veterans would classify them as off-dry if not sweet. The winemakers have sought such a pleasant textural experience, where the wines are rich in flavors, full-bodied, and *distinctly* sweet, they end up with easy drinking, smooth wines. Elitists will frown upon these wines because the masses enjoy them. These are the people who hate Harry Potter and Beyoncé. They hate things that are easily enjoyed. Self-hating masochists, I say. I love Hermione. And surfborts.

#TeachYoMouth Moment: Sweet

Non-wine example: Eat some gummy bears, a slice of watermelon, a scoop of ice cream—do I really have to keep going? This one is easy from a food perspective: we all know and love sweet.

Wine example: *Pacific Rim* is not just a terrible sci-fi movie it's also a low-cost producer of Washington Riesling. The winery happens to offer a perfect case study in sweet. It makes a dry and a sweet Riesling. Two wines, made from the exact same grape from the exact same region, and identical in their BOSS profile, save sweetness.

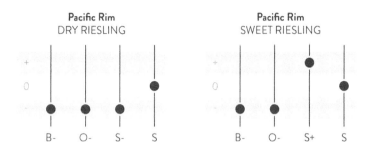

Now let's look at two different red wines with contrasting sweet profiles. Start with the Francis Ford Coppola Claret. *Claret* is a fancy word for a wine blended from the grapes that traditionally make red Bordeaux wines: Cabernet Sauvignon, Cabernet Franc, Merlot, Malbec, and Petit Verdot. In this case, the winery has chosen only Cabernet Sauvignon and Merlot. You'll notice that the wine is full-bodied, oaky, dry, and neutral in its sour profile (B+O+S-S). Now try Apothic Red. It too is full-bodied, oaky, and with a neutral sour profile, but the wine is slightly fuller, rounder, and, wait for it . . . sweeter. The residual sugar is making that wine a lot sweeter and a lot softer in the mouth than the Coppola wine. If you were to go back and take a sip of the Coppola wine, the oak and tannin profile would now feel harsh and astringent after the dollop of dessert that is Apothic Red.

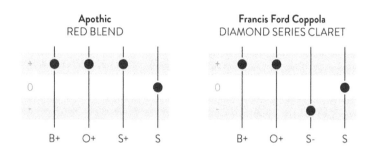

If you have kept up with me this far, you now have learned the first S in BOSS and mastered three of the four concepts of this book. Your stewardess hasn't even given you the go-ahead to turn on your laptop yet, and you have three of four BOSS components checked off.

Sour

Now let's talk about sour, a.k.a., acid. If you have acid reflux, had a bad experience partying in the 1970s, or have a fear of Batman pushing you into a large vat, we need to dispel any confusion about what we are talking about with acid. Sour isn't nearly as precise as acid as a wine descriptor, but honestly, creating a decent acronym was hard and acid just didn't fit in. I iterated so many different synonyms and four-letter acronyms before I started hating the English language and figured we could at least be ironic and share some cheap laughs hashtagging #BEABOSS. So sour it is, and acid it is not.

Your salad dressing, orange juice, and milk—yes, even your milk—contain acid. Acid is present in most of the things you enjoy on a daily basis, and it has a powerful effect on what you eat, drink, and ultimately enjoy. Get comfortable with talking about acid, a.k.a., sour, as it will help you explain the foods and wines you enjoy. At dinnertime, acid adds freshness, vibrancy, or brightness to the meal. What does a squeeze of lime bring to your meaty, savory, greasy carnitas tacos? What does a squeeze of lemon add to a salty, crunchy-skinned, savory roasted chicken? What about the orange in your orange-glazed pork? The effect that citric acid has on your food illustrates the role acid plays in the wines you drink, like the classic high-acid wines New Zealand Sauvignon Blanc, Barbera d'Asti in Piedmont, and Riesling from Mosel. These wines are distinctly sour because of their high acidity. If you have a strong preference for or aversion to these wines, it might be because of their high levels of acid. My dad in particular isn't much of a sparkling wine fan, rarely enjoying even an expensive Champagne. It's the acid that bothers him, the austere effect it has on his stomach. To most palates, these three wines will demonstrate a level of brightness or freshness, whereas wines that lack noticeable acid will be described by the wine douchetocracy as "dull," "muted," or "flabby."

To illustrate, try your meaty tacos with and without the lime. Try roasted chicken with and without the lemon. How different is a grilled skirt steak with and without the chimichurri sauce? Chimichurri is mostly herbs and citrus, both of which lighten up a potentially fatty cut of beef. Without the sour tang, the fattiness of these foods will be more noticeable, possibly to the point of greasiness. Again, the wines I just described have other differentiating qualities, but acid will help us group and separate the wine world.

How do we translate this idea from food to wine? Acid is easily perceived when squeezing citrus on your food, but it's perhaps the most challenging quality to decipher when learning wine. Don't fret; there's a simple trick that will help you, a surefire way to gauge the level of sourness. After you swirl some wine around in your mouth and swallow, wait a moment and notice your gums. Are they watering? Are they watering a lot or not really at all? Your mouth has an automatic reaction to acid; it waters. If you're not sure how acidic the wine is, or what your preference is, simply pay attention to how much your mouth waters. Over time, you'll notice the sour as either missing or perhaps overbearing, depending on your tastes, and you won't need this trick. But for now, this will be a certain approach to successfully gauging the sour or acid in wine.

Acid is also perhaps the most polarizing of the four elements of BOSS. For those who love it, its absence is a glaring weakness in a wine. For those who have no overwhelming preference for it, its absence will not be missed. The more attention you pay to wine, the more you will notice that those who love wine generally settle on one side or the other of this oenological Mason-Dixon Line, and it can get contentious. In any case, what's important for now is that you understand and appreciate how sour shows up in your glass. To that end, please enjoy round four.

#TeachYoMouth Moment: Sour

Non-wine examples: Your salad with just olive oil is slippery and greasy. Now try your salad with olive oil and vinegar and suddenly you'll taste a new level of complexity, engaging new parts of your mouth with a zippy taste and sensation. More simply, notice that tang. That tang is the sour, a.k.a. the acid. The type of vinegar that you use will affect the flavors, but all vinegars will deliver that tang. A rice wine vinegar might be nutty, and a balsamic vinegar will be more like molasses, but they both will be sour.

Wine examples: Don't forget the trick! If you're not sure about the level of sour, wait for your gums to water. Let's start with the Mirassou Pinot Noir. It doesn't have much body, being a typical Pinot Noir. It has a mild oak flavor, no sweetness, and a very sour, juicy level of acidity (B-OS-S+). Contrast that with the Cabernet from Robert Mondavi. It's full-bodied, neutral oak, no sweetness, and very low sour. Your mouth waters less than with the Pinot Noir.

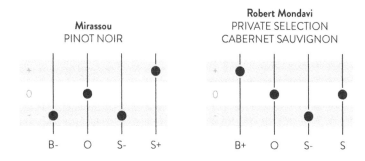

Just like I had a hard time finding a red wine without oak, I had a hard time finding white wines with low levels of acid. I honestly thought this would be easy, but I'm pleased and delighted to say that so many widely distributed white wines have such prominent levels of acid. White wine, without the sour tang of acid, really makes for a boring white wine. But don't misinterpret the implication: just because I couldn't find mass-produced white wines with low levels of sour, it doesn't mean that all white wines have the same level of sour. Using your trick of monitoring salivation, over time you will notice that some white wines are downright juicy, rushing your mouth with saliva, where others with more moderate sour will still make your mouth water just slightly. Again, it comes back to the subtle differences creating the major distinctions. But this red wine tasting clearly demonstrates how acid changes the level of sour with uncontested clarity.

Guess what?

That's it.

That's the whole show.

Those are the four building blocks you need to describe a wine. Those four attributes can summarize every single style of wine produced on this planet. How much more helpful is this than a tasting note? I hope those four concepts are easily *digested* (drink!) in the context of the everyday items you consume.

I said you could stop reading here and get your money's worth, but keep a significant caveat in mind as you take BOSS into the real world. Are you getting tired of my caveats yet? I swear I'm not a total coward; I'm just trying to be as accurate and transparent as I can be.

My biggest fear is that, as you take BOSS out into the real world, you're going to run into barriers, or more accurately, unqualified hacks, witless wonders, or overwhelmed salespersons who purport to be experts. You're going to run into these frauds who sell wine or waiters who push higher-priced wines on you, and they themselves won't know the oak profile or the level of sour in a wine they are pimping. There are plenty of people who profess to know a lot about wine, but really it's their third week on the job at the local wine shop and they can only tell you about the four wines they tasted on their first day. Or, more commonly, these perfectly competent, talented folks just might have to sell dozens if not hundreds of wines, so how could they possibly know the profile of every one?

Don't let that stop you from asking questions about wines, using your BOSS framework, and having conversations about what you like. It is quite likely that you, me, and my mother are the only people who have read this book at the outset, so BOSS may not yet be a well-known thing. However, thinking about your mouth tuner and your preferred wine profiles using the words "body," "oak," "sour," and "sweet" will work with most gatekeepers of wine. I've selected these words knowing that you'd have to take them into the real world when ordering or buying wine. But to be honest, you'll now have a better wine vocabulary than some of these gatekeepers.

Our revolution has to start somewhere, and the thought of you putting these gatekeepers on their heels delights me endlessly. You will force them to become more educated on the wines they sell, further reducing the potential for failure. There will eventually be fewer Joel McHale salespersons in this world. Great comic, terrible wine salesman. Ultimately, you will be dependent upon the brilliant, hardworking people who stock shelves and create wine lists with understanding, a sense of adventure, prescience, and passion. I'm confident these people will outweigh the frauds in your experiences, and you will succeed.

CHAPTER 3

EXPLAINING SOME SCIENCE BEHIND THE MAGIC

*An infinite question is often destroyed by finite answers.
To define everything is to annihilate much that gives us
laughter and joy.*

—Madeleine L'Engle

M y mom once asked, "How do they get all of those flavors into the wine? What additives do they use?" Better yet, what is wine and where does the BOSS come from? My mom's question is a very logical one, especially after hearing a wine chucklehead pine about the beautiful cherry and bright raspberry flavors accented by unicorn kisses and space dust. That logical gap in my mom's mind is the essence of one of the truly great miracles of wine. Wine grapes, in all their wondrous glory, naturally express this complexity. Grapes possess a miraculous array of fruit, vegetable, and other natural flavors. So to my mom, I can say that nothing is added. Whereas your pad Thai gets as delicious as it does by combining peanuts, soy, soy sauce, fish sauce, chicken, lime juice, chiles, and eggs, your Pinot Noir has the natural complexity of black cherries, dried mushrooms, and orange peel all on its own. How cool is that, by the way?

But back to Mom's question, how does all of this wonder manifest?

Winemaking 101

Any alcoholic beverage starts with a natural process: fermentation. Lots of wonderful, hungry, microscopic yeasts live in the wild, especially in vineyards, forests, and farms. When these native microorganisms come into contact with sugar—from grapes, apples, raspberries, anything—they eat the sugar and one of the byproducts is alcohol. This little miracle can happen on a small scale anywhere you see a split piece of fruit, an apple fallen from a tree or grapes split open by a bird or a hailstorm. Naturally, we industrious humans discovered how fantastic all this alcohol stuff was, and we started controlling the fermentation factors so we could produce different types of alcohol, and with consistency. Fermenting grapes creates wine, fermenting cooked grains creates beer (cooking a grain releases its sugars, which would otherwise be locked away as a carbohydrate), and fermenting cooked agave is the beginning of tequila. In fact, you can technically make an alcoholic beverage from anything that contains sugar. But please finish my book before you rush to the pantry to start fermenting your Fruity Pebbles. Unless it's delicious—in which case, please call me immediately.

Only two simple ingredients, then, are needed to produce every alcohol on this planet: sugar and yeast. While the ingredients only number two, it is the combination of the grapes, the growing environment, and only a handful of winemaking techniques that produce every different style of wine that we drink. In other words, the great diversity of wine from around the world doesn't require elaborate processes or extensive chemical studies; their origins are miraculously simple. While it can get more complex with other types of wine, I'm going to deliberately avoid the more convoluted beasts in the wine world for didactic simplicity. Sparkling wines (like Champagne, Franciacorta, and Prosecco) and fortified wines (like Madeira, Port, and Sherry) come from highly evolved, esoteric, and relatively complicated winemaking techniques, whereas the traditional wines we drink every day come from relatively simple techniques. Some very rare dessert wines can even employ mold, ice, or extremely hot conditions for drying out wine grapes. Yes, fine wines can be made from rotten fruit covered in mold, from freezing the water out of the grapes, or from raisined grapes dried out in the sun. While these sound like things you're more likely to see in Chinatown earning a "D" rating from the health department, they're actually winemaking techniques that extract moisture and concentrate flavors, creating some of the most expensive wines on the planet and many of my favorites. They are also not a great starting point for wine education, since their deliciousness and expense are explained by a tremendous amount of varying steps and nuances, region by region, winemaker by winemaker. It's horribly boring if you don't really care (though exhilarating if you do).

While the natural fermentation phenomenon I just described is simple, in the modern era we clearly are more deliberate in producing our alcohol. We can't wait for birds and hailstorms to get our drink on. For a red wine, we first crush the grapes and let them stew in their juices. For white wines, we press the juice out of the grapes to minimize contact with the skins of the grapes. Why the different techniques? We'll cover this in more detail later, but for now, let's just say we don't want the skins of white grapes soaking in the juice.

Whether crushed and stewed or pressed from the grapes, this extracted juice or "must" is very drinkable grape juice at this point. However, the difference between this juice and Welch's grape juice is certainly noticeable; it's because the grapes are different species. Welch's Concord grapes are native to the States and really don't make pleasant wines. The grape varieties that are native to Europe and have come to dominate the wine landscape are more complex in flavor. Have you ever had jam made from Napa Valley Cabernet grapes? It's pretty tasty stuff. As we learned from Ben Stiller in *Meet the Parents*, you can milk a cat, but you'd probably prefer the milk of cows, goats, and sheep. Different species and genera offer different characteristics. In short, with traditional European grape varieties, you're starting with a unique grape to create this unique grape juice.

Nowadays, we rely less and less on native yeasts that exist in the vineyard to do the heavy lifting of fermentation. We have learned to cultivate winemaker-friendly yeasts. Crest has its whitening toothpaste and Starbucks makes a chestnut praline latte. In wine, we have cultivated yeasts. These yeasts can add some complexity and character, but, most importantly, they ensure a fermentation process without surprises. Native, wild yeasts are more uncontrollable in the winery and can produce inconsistent results. One more thing about fermenting: If you let the yeast ferment the grape juice in an open vat, you will get a standard "still" wine.

Ferment it under pressure in a closed tank, you trap the carbon dioxide—the second byproduct of the yeasts eating the sugar—and you make a sparkling wine.

I will pause here for applause. Thank you, France, for making brunch extraordinary with this modest innovation. There is some debate on who the true inventor of Champagne is, but my guess is that like most things, bubbles in wine was a known potential outcome, but it wasn't what people wanted, so people didn't deliberately repeat the steps to make it a marketable product. That is, until Dom Pérignon and others found a place for it.

In any case, bubbles or not, fermentation continues until all of the yeasts have spent themselves, converting all of the sugar to ethanol (alcohol), and then dying. Ethanol is the "safe" alcohol that comes from fermentation. If so inclined, you can layer on additional steps to turn a wine or fermented beverage into a spirit, the process known as distillation. Distillation is the perfect word for the process, as you are quite literally concentrating the alcohol and removing the filler. Distill wine, and you'll have brandy. Distill beer, you'll get whisky. A more sinister alcohol you get when distilling any fermented alcohol is methanol. At least once a month, it seems, some yahoos in the far reaches of India try to distill whisky and don't know how to extract the deadly methanol from the ethanol and they kill people. This is why moonshining sometimes isn't amazing.

But these are the processes that create the beverages we love, described simply.

By the time the yeasts have eaten all the sugar and died, the wine finally resembles wine more than it does grape juice, although it is pretty yeasty in flavor. Imagine wine marinated in sourdough bread. It's not gross, but it's not delicious. Give it some time to rest, to age, and it will achieve bliss. For most wines, the juice is emptied from the fermentation tanks into an oak barrel, where the months spent aging will mellow it out into the complex euphoria that is wine. The yeastiness dies down, and the natural complexity of the wine emerges. If the wine isn't going to be aged in oak, as with a Sancerre, Italian Pinot Grigio, or New Zealand Sauvignon Blanc, you skip the final step, and allow the wines to rest and find glory in neutral, stainless-steel tanks.

Why are so many whites aged in neutral vessels instead of oak? Believe it or not, aging white wines in neutral vessels instead of oak barrels is a more recent innovation, given the timeline of winemaking that reaches back to antiquity. Stainless steel fermentation wasn't even common until the renowned French winemaker, Emile Peynaud, began advocating for it in the 1960s to afford winemakers greater control in the winemaking process. Introducing a new flavor, like oak, can make something more complex, but it also can dilute the impact of any one of the other ingredients. Think of it as deciding between a margherita pizza and a meat lover's pizza. In making a white wine, a winemaker can decide to let the pure, refreshing aromatics that exist in the wine shine, just as the simplicity and aromatic bliss of basil, mozzarella, and fresh tomato achieve deliciousness in a margherita pizza. Conversely, a winemaker can choose to beef up a wine by aging it in oak barrels. You might have a personal preference for one of these types of pizza, but it's difficult to argue that one is better than the other; they're just different. It's the winemaker's choice to make the style of wine he wants. We'll discuss more about this shortly.

We have just covered the art of winemaking.

That's it; that's the entire process. Now, I can, and will, complicate this with the decisions that a winemaker is faced with, but first you must understand the simple version—the glorious, basic process that produces the beverage that hooked Romans thousands of years ago and somehow found its way into something as routine as Sunday Mass. How great would church be, by the way, if Padre upgraded the vino? In any case, hopefully you now trust me that you can learn the science without much trouble. We aren't finished, however, until we understand where the BOSS comes from. The basic fermentation process doesn't change, but we will discuss a handful of factors that create the vast range of nuances, distinct characters, and BOSS profiles of all the world's wines.

BOSSmaking 101

If sugar in grapes feeds the yeast to produce alcohol, it naturally follows that the more sugar in a grape, the more potential alcohol in a wine. Why does this sugar-alcohol relationship matter? The level of alcohol in your wine has a dramatic effect on the wine in your mouth. As I mentioned earlier, alcohol creates weight, a.k.a. body. Remember that a low-alcohol wine and a high-alcohol wine will have the same difference in weight that skim milk and whole milk do. But know that we're not talking about a vast difference in alcohol content; we're actually talking about differences of 1 or 2 percent alcohol by volume. As I've mentioned, it is the subtle differences that create the major distinctions in wine. So it is for the differences in alcohol.

It should not surprise us then that the big-body wines of Rioja, Barossa Valley, and Napa Valley achieve their girth from having a higher percentage of sugar in their grapes. That sugar is then converted to a higher percentage of alcohol. This is in contrast to the wines of the Willamette Valley, Alsace, and Pfalz, where we find less sugar in the grapes. Is it a coincidence that these last three places all have much cooler climates? Nope. All things being equal, the warmer the climate, the riper the grapes get, and that means more sugar. Smash a grape from the Antarctic current-blasted islands of New Zealand in your fingers and there will be less sugar in the juice than in the grapes from the sun-baked slopes of the Côte Rôtie in Southern France, a region whose name literally translates into "roasted slopes." A warmer climate creates riper, higher-sugar fruit, which in turn creates more alcohol, which gives you (boom) more "B" in your BOSS. In short, warmer climates express themselves in your glass of wine as higher-alcohol, bigger-body wines.

The other major source of "B" is oak. The oak barrels in which the wine is aged not only add the flavors of the oak, they release tannin compounds and impart a heavier weight, extracting wood sugars, hemicelluloses, and kisses from tiny fairies. But as we've discussed, the most important effects of oak-aging wine are the release of tannin and oak flavor, followed closely by this whole evaporation thing.

Evaporation is a powerful agent in producing everything from rum to whisky to wine, and the conditions under which your preferred booze is aged has a profound impact on the final product. Distillers in Kentucky can expect to lose half of their whisky to evaporation over four years. In Scotland, you might only lose a quarter. Ever wonder why tequilas aren't aged for nearly as long as whisky? The heat of Mexico would leave you without any hooch to sell. Significant differences in evaporation rates result from geographic differences in heat and humidity, the more of which accelerates evaporation. The "angel's share," as evaporation has long been called, has the effect of concentrating the components that are least prone to evaporating—the yummy bits—creating a reduction that translates into body and weight (i.e., like the whole milk).

What's amazing is that you can taste the same wine from the same vineyard, one aged in oak, one not, and not only will you have wine with different flavors, but also different texture and weight. They, in fact, will taste like two totally different wines!

To those who are averse to heavy oak flavors, a wine aged in brand new oak barrels for a year can feel like a heavy hand. This is the profile that the Chardonnays of Napa Valley have become famous for: big old oak monsters. While this reputation isn't exactly fair, this intense oak regimen will make the oak flavors and textures more pronounced. You might see a wine that is aged "50 percent in new oak," and that means that only half of the wine, before all lots from all the vineyards and tanks were blended together and bottled, was aged in new oak barrels.

This more moderate oak regimen creates a wine with more subtle oak flavors and lower body. What they are not telling you about the other 50 percent is not sinister but perhaps confusing. That other 50 percent of the wine was aged in neutral, stainless-steel tanks or in oak barrels that have already been used, and often to the point that the barrels have lost their ability to impart any oak flavors to the wine. After a barrel is used once, its ability to impart oak flavors and weight is diminished by roughly half. Another use would reduce the impact of the oak by another half, and so on. Why bother using these barrels if they aren't imparting any significant flavor? Because you still get the benefits of evaporation and some very small oxygenation that shape and settle the wine, the aging that takes you from wine marinated in sourdough bread to the beverage you know and love.

We've discussed that the oak sensation, at its most basic level, is a bitter flavor and is no different from the bitterness that comes from an espresso or from brussels sprouts. Some like it in wine; some do not. Some don't mind the bitter taste, but may not appreciate the serious butter flavor that you smell and taste in white wine. Others love the butter and find wines without it uninteresting. Some, like myself, appreciate it where it fits in with their food or occasion. To those who don't like it, I tell you to grab a bag of salty potato chips and knock the top off an oak monster. That philistine pairing befits the gods.

There is another more calculated reason to apply a serious oak regimen. Sure, it can make for that style of buttery Chardonnay that some love, but the very rare, long-aged wines of this planet, like wines from Bordeaux and Barolo, also see extended oak aging, spending up to two years in a barrel. These aren't wines made to be drunk soon after their release because they have this very intense oak flavor and oak tannin. These wines achieve their pinnacle after the oak characteristics have softened, which will happen as the wine collects years in the bottle. That desiccation and intense dryness from the tannin quite literally soften and the textures become friendly. These rare wines are designed to be aged, and they can be delicious for decades because the tannin that would wound your gums in the first few years after bottling protects the wines for years to come, allowing the fruity complexity to subsist along the way. Makes sense, right? The same compound that protects a plant from rot and disease also protects a wine as it ages.

I read an article that quoted Grant Reynolds, wine director at hot spot New York restaurant Charlie Bird, where he succinctly describes the young Barolo experience: "I don't mind abrasive tannin. It's the nature of the wines. But you have to have the right food with it." Many people adore oak for its punch-to-the-mouth desiccation that strips your lips and gums of moisture. Many believe it requires a juicy, dry-aged, and well-seasoned prime rib. Or a porterhouse with lots of salt and pepper, maybe some freshly grated horseradish. How about a tender slice of skirt steak, with big crunches of sea salt? Give me a moment as I wipe the drool off my keyboard. Big oak flavor and tannin can be intense early in the life of these wines, but they soften with age and can be tempered with the right food. Wait for chapter 4 to make perfect sense of this.

What a great time to set the record straight about drinking old, rare, and often expensive wine. In the February 19, 2015 edition of the *Financial Times*, I saw two bottles of 1945 Château Mouton Rothschild selling for over £5,000 at auction. The record for the most expensive bottle ever sold was $232,692 for a wine made in 1869. What was the wine? Who cares? This could have been a scholarship fund. More importantly, it is not 38,782 times better than a bottle of Yellow Tail Shiraz. Supply and demand dictate that rare things can fetch high prices. But what is the wine like? Is it more delicious?

I once read a quote from one of my favorite industry characters, André Tchelistcheff: "Drinking old wine is like making love to an old woman. You can do it, you might even enjoy it, but it requires a wee bit of imagination." André is one of the founding fathers of modern Napa wine, having worked for the Latour family at Beaulieu Vineyards in the 1970s. André passed away before I started in the wine business. A few, more senior colleagues of mine have insightful, hilarious, and perhaps offensive stories from André, a man capable of perfectly intertwining wit and wisdom. What does his quote mean?

Old wines are not necessarily better. To be sure, few wines improve with age—only a very rare, select few in fact. Drinking old wines in this rare club is therefore a special experience. By special, I don't mean exclusive; I mean that it requires a certain set of circumstances. Old wine requires context. If you don't know how the wine tasted in its youth, or if you don't understand how similar wines taste and change over time, you are likely to miss the point. This is why old wine tastings are done as "verticals" or "horizontals." A vertical tasting is a flight of the same wine from different vintages. A horizontal tasting is a flight of like wines from different producers, but all from the same vintage.

Drinking old wine in these contexts is fun because, as in the case of a vertical, you can imagine how a wine ages. It's like looking at a wine's scrapbook from infancy, through grade school into high school, college, midlife crisis, and old age. You come to appreciate the wine at that point in its life, understanding how sprightly it still is or perhaps how decrepit it has become. A horizontal tasting shows you how different producers make choices about their winemaking and how the characteristics of different vineyard sites create different profiles in the wine even though they're from the same vintage. These two approaches are the best way to understand these rare wines, and it's how we in the industry objectively evaluate the quality of wines. We taste wines against their peers, and see who stands out. In either case, like Andre said, it requires imagination. Or more specifically, it requires understanding or imagining context. When people without this context brag about drinking old, expensive wines to make other people feel inferior, I naturally imagine them bragging about having sex with old ladies. Disgusting perverts, these people.

Where are my white wine drinkers? Many of you may like oaky Chardonnay, but some still prefer the delicate, subtle nuances of Sancerre, Gewürtztraminer, or Chablis. As we discussed, these latter wines aren't commonly aged in oak, nor are they regularly soaked on their skins after the grapes are crushed, as red wines are. These white wines are pressed from the grapes, immediately separated from their skins, and fermented and aged in stainless steel tanks, which is effectively a neutral vessel, imparting no flavors to the wine. Why the different measures for these white wines? First, stainless steel allows the delicate aromatics to be preserved. Oak would overpower the fragile, subtle characteristics of these wines. Second, if white wine juice was allowed to soak on their skins, the wine would pick up the tannins and the earthier flavors of the skins—instead of releasing fragrant, fresh, and fruity characteristics. For these unoaked wines, the "O" is, now perhaps obviously, nonexistent.

To summarize the ground we have just covered in eight pages, the "B" in BOSS can come from the alcohol, which comes from the amount of sugar in the grape, and it can come from the oak barrels in which wine is aged. It should go without saying then that a wine not aged in oak will, all things being equal, be lighter-bodied than its counterpart aged in oak. The "O" only comes from the oak barrels.

Congratulations! You have now earned your "B" and "O" merit badges! You are on your way to being a BOSS. Rick Ross probably wouldn't be okay with merit badges, but remember, he was once a correctional officer.

Sweet and Sour

Let's now understand another source of the BOSS: the sweetness, our first "S." We know that alcohol comes from the amount of sugar in a grape, so it naturally follows then that, during fermentation, a winemaker has the option of creating a sweet wine by stopping fermentation before the yeasts have digested all of the sugar. Interrupting fermentation not only leaves some residual sugar in the wine, but it also keeps the alcohol content low. This happens in the delightful off-dry or sweet wines of the Loire Valley, Alsace, and Germany. Another class of more affordable, sweet wine that's available on store shelves across this great country uses a different approach. These lower-cost wines derive sweetness from the addition of sugar, using a method no more glamorous or romantic than adding Sweet 'N Low to your iced tea. Whether your sugar is added or residual from interrupted fermentation, you will notice more "S" in your BOSS profile for sweetness.

So here's another quick cheat for understanding what we have just covered. Climate impacts the sugar level in grapes, and the winemaker decides what to do with that sugar: either let fermentation remove all of it, or allow some to linger—a decision that affects both the alcohol content and body ("B") and its degree of sweetness ("S").

One "S" left: let's talk sour. As we covered earlier, sour comes from acid. The level of acid in a wine, like sugar, is primarily derived from the climate in which the grapes grow. Some grape varieties genetically have more or less acid, but it's climate first and foremost that affects acid content. Those Antarctic currents that slam cold air into New Zealand and keep sugar low also keep acid high.

As a grape ripens during a vintage, its acid naturally declines as its sugar naturally rises. Finding the exact moment in the growing season when you have the Goldilocks amount of sugar and acid is a winemaker's challenge. "Optimal ripeness" is the day of the year when the winemaker believes he has achieved the ideal mix of acid and sugar, and grapes are pulled from the vine. All things being equal, pull the grapes down early, and you will have low sugar ("S") and high acid ("S"). Pull late, and the reverse will be true. Pull when these elements are in balance, and you will have some tasty porridge.

The natural acid differences in grapes can also assert themselves. For example, Sauvignon Blanc grapes are naturally higher in acid than are Merlot grapes. These genetic differences in the grape have evolved over time, and they are no different than the different color hair or sizes of you and your siblings.

You have just graduated to a new level of wine understanding. Not only do you understand where each component of BOSS comes from, but with what you have now read, you can articulately address what we in the industry call "old world wines" versus "new world wines." For years, and this is perhaps overly general, the leading wine production regions of Europe have had cooler climates than the leading wine production regions of California, Australia, and South America. You now know that those cooler climates tend to create lighter-bodied, lower-alcohol, and higher-acid wines (B-OSS+). The warmer climates tend to create higher-alcohol, bigger-bodied, lower-acid wines (B+OSS-). That's old world versus new world in a nutshell.

Why is this helpful? First, it can simply divide the world and all of its wine into two major groups. More importantly, if you find you prefer one of these styles, you can more easily navigate to wines you like on a menu or with the counsel of a retail wine steward. This climate distinction has been such a consistent, observable wine feature that "old world" and "new world" permeate the lexicon of those in the industry and is how we veterans have grown up learning about wines.

Over time, however, this black-and-white difference has grayed. We've seen producers from both "worlds" emulate the profiles of the other. We've seen producers on the right bank of Bordeaux achieve new-world style wines under the *garagistes* movement, and we've seen many California producers produce low-alcohol, lighter-bodied wines under the banner of a group called "In Pursuit of Balance." What would compel a producer to buck the trends of its neighbors and operate outside the norms that have been cultivated over decades or even centuries?

Most people have a preference for one world or the other, so it's effectively a business decision by the winery to target a different group of wine drinkers or simply champion a wine style in which they fervently believe. I personally adore both worlds, but probably lean toward one for most occasions. In either case, people can generally describe themselves as liking one type or another, perhaps if only for a certain occasion, and it will be helpful to determine on which side you reside. This is one of the simplest ways to describe what you like to a somm or wine shop attendant: old world or new.

You now see that the BOSS differences in wine come only from the winemaking techniques employed, the genetic makeup of the grapes, and the natural environment in which the grapes grow. Those three simple factors create all the wondrous diversity in wine. Perhaps surprisingly, it is the third factor that can separate good wine from great wine and creates the truly infinite possibilities for a grape. Far more than winemaking techniques and genetic makeup, the habitat of the grapes defines the character and potential of a wine, what the French call *terroir*. And you must love the French: they created the concept of *terroir*. It was marketing before there was marketing. My French friends assure me there is no literal translation for *terroir*, but is approximated best by a "sense of place." It is meant to describe all of the known and unknown factors in a growing area that contribute to the complexity and character of a wine. This includes but is not limited to the chemical content of the soil, the structure of the soil at different depths and its ability to drain and retain water, the climate of the region, the temperature and sunlight exposure under the canopies of the vines, the direction of the rows in relation to the sun, the temperature swing from day to night, and the slope and height of the vineyard.

Wine is one of those things often described as an art and a science, but in the vineyard at least, I tend to think of the art as the unknown science, and *terroir* is the complicated science we can't yet completely measure, understand, or articulate. To the French, the unique vineyard plots that comprise a wine are the mystery and romance that is *terroir*. You have to channel your inner Parisian, under a full moon on a summer night, with a beautiful young someone across an exquisitely set table, glass of wine in hand, staring into each other's eyes, and say it with me . . . terr-WAH (and make it nasal).

No matter what we call it, complex environmental factors create wonderfully distinct wine profiles. The winemaker can use an exact genetic clone of a grape in two different places in a vineyard, mere yards apart, treat them with the exact same winemaking techniques, and end up with fundamentally different wines, simply because of the unique and minute *terroir* differences of those sites. Tiny miracles are the best.

CHAPTER 4

FINDING GOD: FOOD AND WINE PAIRING

I don't stop eating when I'm full. The meal is not over when I'm full. The meal is over when I hate myself.
—**Louis C.K.**, from *Chewed Up*, 2008

F or me, wine is a cover. My true love is food. Quite a few folks in the wine business are foodies disguised as wine geeks. For me, a wine hasn't unlocked its potential until it is matched with the right food. The right meal with the right wine isn't just a trivial, gluttonous, and fleeting moment for people lacking real-life problems; it is also a journey through space and time to connect with peoples, cultures, and foods that have grown up together over the centuries.

Is it a coincidence that Albariño from Rías Baixas goes famously with the seafood found off the nearby coasts? Can it be that the acorn-fed, salty, and savory *jamón ibérico* of Spain just happens to match spectacularly with the silky, fruity, oaky wines of Rioja? Humans might have cultivated the grapes of these regions because they were well suited to the climate and soil of the Iberian peninsula, but you can't deny the possibility that these wines thrive in these regions today at least in part because of the remarkable union the wine achieves with the local food culture. Having simply prepared fish with Portuguese Alvarinho is not only a tried-and-true pairing for your dinner tonight; it is an experience perfected by a culture and community of fishermen, wineries, and hardworking human beings who have lived their lives a certain way for decades or centuries. Think of your meal tonight as a communal ritual that has transpired millions of times, over thousands of years, across myriad cultures, families, traditions, and life events. What a rare, shared human connection.

And why has this ritual repeated itself so many times? 'Cause it tastes good. Even if you don't geek out on the transcendent, cultural, time-travel experience, I imagine you can get onboard with the simple, tasty pleasure of pairing food and wine. Putting a great wine with great cuisine changes the entire meal. Even paired poorly, wine will always elevate your meal. Paired well, food will reveal nuances of the wine that will fire new synapses in your brain, animate previously dormant taste buds, and probably cure cancer.

But be warned: while food can, in a brilliant way, show you a version of your wine that you never knew existed, it can also, in a troublesome way, corrupt your perception of a wine. Food and wine pairing then, simply, is about avoiding the latter and creating an opportunity for the former.

As you will read in another chapter, much of my love of wine stems from the love of the people who make it. The many people who labor 365 days a year, and the many people who have labored over the course of a few thousand years, make wine what it is today. Similarly, this chapter wouldn't be possible without one brilliant man who taught me much about enjoying food and wine. I hope many in the wine business would agree that this man has uncovered more insightful lessons and taught more people in the industry how to be successful with food and wine pairing than anyone else. Jerry Comfort of the Beringer Winery is a brilliant trailblazer with food and wine pairing, and I would be remiss not to thank him here for the many lessons he has taught so many in the industry over the years, myself included. Next time through Napa, experience his seminar for yourself.

Stanky Cheese Symphony

I was at a happy hour recently with colleagues at this lovely bistro that had two vintages of a Muscadet Sèvre et Maine (B-O-S-S+). I asked the barkeep to pour both vintages side by side to see who preferred the 2009 versus the 2011. The 2011 was bright, fresh, and fruity, and the 2009 was funky and dusty, like stale sourdough bread and stinky cheese. Everyone categorically picked the 2011. Except me. Why would anyone like this funky profile in a wine? Nobody in his right mind would pick this wine as it was. I, however, was imagining the stanky blue cheese that would change this wine from the challenging assault to the senses to the decadent pairing that would bring them to their knees. Food can help make sense of a wine.

Sometimes when I dine, I hear a waiter say something along the lines of: "The earthiness in the mushroom pasta will pair well with the earthiness of this Pinot Noir from the Willamette Valley." Sure, you can pair food and wine based on two common flavors and nothing else, but you're not accomplishing much.

First, the flavors are actually smells. So one problem with this most common approach is that you are not necessarily accounting for the tastes in your mouth. Recall that salty, sweet, sour, bitter, and umami are what your mouth detects, not the aroma of mushrooms. It is more important that we account for the tastes in food pairing than the flavors you are smelling. The second and more important problem is your mouth's acclimation to the tastes in your food.

In the freezing temperatures of winter, have you ever had to come inside and wash your hands? If you've spent a considerable amount of time outside, do you turn on the hot water right away? Of course not! More likely, you find a lukewarm temperature. Why do we do this? Hot water is painful because you haven't acclimated to the warmer temperature in the house yet. At that moment, washing your hands in what you would normally consider "cold water" is actually pleasant because you've just come in from freezing temperatures and that "cold water" is still warmer than the temperature outside—unless you live in Southern California, in which case nobody wants to hear about it. More to the point, your skin had already acclimated to the cold outside, but couldn't adjust quickly enough to hot water on your hands inside. The dramatic swing the hot water on your hands presents is downright shocking to your sense of touch.

Perhaps not surprisingly then, your taste buds' acclimation to food and wine is no different than temperature acclimation is for your skin. Start eating that mushroom pasta and your mouth will acclimate to those flavors, so much so that everything but the earthy flavors of the wine is what you will notice when you taste the wine. Acclimation is perhaps the most essential effect to account for with food and wine pairing. We'll taste how this happens.

I was counting on the effect of acclimation when I imagined the stanky blue cheese I wanted to eat with that old Muscadet. Match their funkiness together and you will see beauty and tastiness emerge, like that of a pickleback shot. The other characteristics in the wine that you didn't notice before because of the overwhelming funk begin to assert themselves. A fundamentally different wine reveals itself. With how many other experiences or disciplines can you enjoy this phenomenon like you do in wine? Where else do two sins create symphony?

Offal Joy

I have five rules to guarantee your food and wine happiness, five #TeachYoMouth moments that will ensure we deliver on the Hippocratic Oath. Read quickly, these rules are somewhat boring, trite, and the opposite of the transcendent experience I promised. But as before, we will taste-test these rules so that you understand them intuitively, taking you from an elementary appreciation of the concepts to a visceral epiphany that will ensure your own personal "hallelujah" moments with food and wine for years to come.

As we dive in, things will of course be simpler because you have a foundation as a BOSS. It also gets easier because, as you know, the "body" in BOSS isn't a taste. So we are afforded the luxury of focusing on the three tastes in your wine (oak, sweet, and sour) and their interaction with food. Knowing how the five tastes that can be present in your food interact with the three tastes that can be present in your wine, then, is our task. In short, the rules will manage the effects of acclimation in your mouth to prevent food crimes against wine. I'll give you the list of rules up front, and then we will #TeachYoMouth, rule by rule.

When choosing your food before your wine, make sure: (1) sweet food gets a sweet wine, (2) sour food gets a sour wine, and (3) spicy food gets a sweet wine. When choosing your wine before your food, make sure: (4) oaked wines get salty food and (5) neutral wines get neutral food.

Understanding why these rules exist is important if you want to explore and pair freely. Simply following these rules will keep you from blaming a wine for sucking, when really it was the overwhelming food with which you paired it. You, again, could stop here with this simple list of rules and move on with your life knowing that you have minimized the chance of ruining a wine with your entrée selection. Alternatively, you can read on, taste, and understand why these things are the way they are. The following #TeachYoMouth moments are, in effect, switching back and forth between the cold air and the hot water on your hands, but with food and wine in your mouth. We're going to acclimate your mouth to different tastes and see how food and wine interact.

Your grocery list is simple, and perhaps you have everything in your home already: a small bag of salty potato chips, lettuce or a simple salad mix, a vinaigrette salad dressing, some strawberries, and a jalapeño.

This shopping list need not be so rigid, so if you need some alternatives, know that a lemon, lime, or even a bottle of lemon juice will do just as well as salad dressing. Strawberries can be substituted with a sweet red apple, kiwi, watermelon, or any sweet piece of fruit. If a jalapeño is too much to bear or challenging to locate, you can use black pepper (perhaps best for those who are highly sensitive to spicy flavors), pepperoni, hot sauce, or any spicy pepper.

If you don't have potato chips in your house, well, I'm sad for you, but other lovely salty alternatives for our purposes include pretzels, French fries, salted peanuts or cashews, or tortilla chips.

Your wine list is simple as well: a dry unoaked white wine, a dry oaked red wine, and a sweet white wine. From your previous shopping, the Italian Pinot Grigio, the California Cabernet, and the sweet Riesling will all work fine.

#TeachYoMouth Moment: Sweet Foods

The reckless endangerment of wine due to sweet dishes is perhaps the most frequent wine-pairing crime. Sweet foods have a powerful effect on your wine, and being aware of this will unlock new pleasures with the wines you love and help avoid a wine catastrophe. The trouble is that sweet foods don't just arrive with dessert; so many barbecues, sauces, glazes, and braises during the main event are sweet.

All things being equal, sweetness in your food will elevate the non-sweet tastes in your wine. Again, it's the principle of acclimation. With sweet food lingering on your tongue, the bitter oak and sour tastes will assert themselves, and as you would expect, dialing up bitter and sour makes your wine less pleasant.

Start with the white wine. Get to know it, swirl it around in your mouth, and mentally check off the BOSS profile as you take a couple tastes. Hey, if it's Saturday night, take a few big swigs. Now take a bite of your strawberry, and then go back and sip the wine.

Notice a difference? The wine should seem quite a bit harsher as the sour of the wine begins to dominate what you taste. Repeat the exercise by acclimating to the red wine and then tasting the strawberry. Now go back to the red wine and notice how the bitter sensation from the oak dominates the wine.

That sweetness, that pleasant sensation present in so many entrees and desserts, really can rough up your fragile wine. A wine you tasted when the waiter first brought you a glass, a wine you loved and didn't know how you were going to live without, has changed. Sure, he was all charming and nice on the first date, but after a few weeks he's on the couch without pants playing Xbox until four o'clock in the morning. The wine didn't change because you loved it too much and didn't give it enough space; the sweetness in the food brought out an entirely different side of the wine.

What to do? Ban sweet foods from our diets? No more crème brûlée? No more maple-glazed bacon from Landhaus? Are you mad? The solution of course is drinking a wine sweeter than the food itself. Get to know your ports, Sauternes, ice wines, PX Sherry, Moscato d'Asti, and your off-dry Rieslings, Pinot Gris, and Gewürztraminer from Washington or Germany. This bastion of wine so undiscovered by most American consumers is a rich landscape, from floral and delicate to hearty and powerful, no different than the range you see in dry wines. Take a swig of the Riesling and let your mouth acclimate. Then try the strawberry and return to your sweet Riesling. The wine doesn't change much, does it? If anything, you might notice the other complexities in the wine more, now that the sweetness in the wine has been suppressed a bit.

I realize that many people really don't like sweet wines. For those of you who despise sweet wines, I'm not saying you have to start exclusively drinking sweet wines with your meals. But my guess is that if you try them with sweet foods, you will see these wines in a new light and potentially come to appreciate what sweet wines offer. And as you now know, your mouth will first acclimate to the sweet foods you're eating, tempering the sweetness in the wine and bringing out all the other rich flavors and tastes.

If you still fear sweet wines, a safe alternative could just be ordering up some side dishes that aren't sweet to transition you back to the wine you otherwise love. Just be aware that sweet foods will change how your wine tastes. Don't blame the wine for changing.

#TeachYoMouth Moment: Sour Foods

Try that dry white wine first: take a sip, swirl it around, and gulp it down. Take another; let your mouth get used to the wine. Notice its body, its lack of oak, its lack of sweetness, and its level of sour by how much your mouth waters (B-O-S-S+). Now dress your lettuce or salad with your vinaigrette and take a bite. Notice the effect of the acid from the salad dressing in your mouth and register your mouth puckering. Now go back to that white wine and take a sip.

What's different? Do you notice that the wine is softer, probably fruitier? Notice I didn't say sweeter, I said *fruitier*. There is no sugar in the wine, so the salad dressing can't create sweetness. But it can make the other tastes and flavors more apparent. Whereas the citrus flavors were prominent in your wine before, they are now hidden by your mouth's acclimation to the vinaigrette. The strong, mouth-puckering salad dressing has also changed how prominent the acid is in your wine. What was noticeably sour before is now less tangy.

Repeat that exercise with the red wine. Acclimate your mouth to the red wine, swirl it around, and get a sense of its BOSS profile (B+O+S-S). Take a couple sips to ensure you're acclimated. Now have some dressed salad and return to the wine. How soft does the wine feel in your mouth? How heightened are the brooding flavors of the red wine in your mouth? If your red wine was low in sour, you might actually be missing that acid in your wine. Depending on how singularly and powerfully sour your vinaigrette is, your wine might need more sour to stand up to it.

Why are we eating salad and tangy salad dressing? The salad dressing is representative of all the acids that make themselves apparent in your food, like the citrus glaze on your pork, the lemon you squeeze on freshly shucked oysters, and a citrus-soaked ceviche. Wherever you see acid, vinegar, or citrus fruits in a dish, be prepared to experience muted acid from the wines you are drinking. Your strategy, then, is to pick wines with robust acid to ensure your wines don't cower in the face of these powerfully sour dishes or ingredients. As you begin ordering small plates and starters, be aware that dishes with high degrees of sour will be better suited with a wine that's sour. It's always great to start a meal with a glass of old-world white wine to handle fresh seafood appetizers and your fresh, tangy salad.

#TeachYoMouth Moment: Spicy Foods

Spicy is the Comcast of food and wine pairing: it screws up everything. Don't get me wrong, spicy is awesome (the same cannot be said for Comcast). Whether subtle heat from red pepper flakes in your Bolognese or a slap in the face from habanero-torched chili, spicy is a fun and necessary part of eating. But pairing it with wine is a bit of a challenge. If I were honest, I would say the best wine pairing with spicy food is beer, but hey, I'm writing a book on wine, so here we go!

Spicy foods inflame your mouth, and often that heat lingers well after the food has been swallowed. As the sweet and sour in the previous two rules made the other tastes more prominent, the spicy tastes will make the sweet, sour, and oak (bitter) all more apparent. You've probably heard some experts say that big hearty foods like barbecue and spicy Chinese food need big hearty wines, like California Zinfandel or Australian Shiraz (B+O+S-S+). They would say that wines need this level of body, oak, and sour to cope with the assault of spicy foods. To me, this is nothing short of madness.

All that spicy is going to rough up your mouth like sandpaper to wood, leaving your mouth raw for the tannin and acid of the wine. All the nuance, complexities, and flavors will be forgotten, as the strong BOSS tastes in the wine give your mouth a beating.

I have only one wine solution for spicy food: sweet wines. Sweet wines provide that satiation, that wet, lush, and tongue-coating relief, not unlike Preparation H. Yes, I just compared Château d'Yquem to hemorrhoid cream. Although to be fair, this doesn't mean that sweet wines will make the spiciness go away; sweet is not a fire extinguisher. In all likelihood the heat will linger in your mouth. But a sweet wine won't add injury to injury, and more importantly, the wine will remain true to what it is. Remember, "first, do no harm." The spiciness won't overpower the acid, sugar, and other flavors of the wine; all of those things will in fact elevate and stand out. Let's taste to find out.

Depending on your pain threshold for heat, try a bite of the jalapeño (or a taste of the black pepper or another substitute listed). Give your mouth a second to go from the initial fruity and floral notes to the spicy, assertive heat of this hot pepper. Now try the Cabernet. Not much fun, right? That Cabernet is dry and harsh, and the fruity, delightful flavors are far from apparent. In short, everything you might like about that wine is now gone. Not a great pairing. Assuming you still have some residual heat in your mouth, now try the sweet Riesling. How different is the experience? Does that wine hold true to what it is? Does it provide some relief to the bang of the spicy food on your mouth? That is a pairing that will keep you from faulting the wine for a bad experience.

While I appreciate that most people don't swoon for sweet wines in the fine dining environment, I believe that more people would appreciate sweet wines *more* in the context of the right cuisine. Pad Thai, with its complex blend of flavors and tastes, including spicy, is a great complement to a complex and slightly sweet Pinot Gris from the Pacific Northwest. Sweet and spicy barbecue dishes are glorious with sweet, tawny ports. A Sauternes with a $12 bowl of spicy tan tan noodles from Han Dynasty? Probably my death-row meal.

Now, this is where we flip the script. The first three rules help you find wines for the food you were inevitably going to eat—rules to help make the best of a yummy food situation. What if you *really* like Chardonnay? What if it's Argentine Malbec and nothing else for you? What if you really aren't as adventurous with wine as I've assumed for the first three rules, and you're not willing to change the wine you love to fit the cuisine? What if you want to pick your wine? Or what if that's all there is in the house?

I have good news for you: you could in fact forget the first three rules and just follow the next two. You don't have to give up the wines you love; you won't have to drink things you wouldn't otherwise drink, but if you want your chosen wine to keep you as happy as it normally would, you will need to follow two simple rules. Onward.

#TeachYoMouth Moment: Salty Foods

As we've discussed, oak in a wine is, pure and simple, a bitter taste. There are two ways people deal with bitter. You either balance it with sugar or, perhaps surprisingly, you diminish it with salt. Adding sugar to your coffee or hazelnut syrup to your latte is clearly the former. But far less common is the practice of using salt to tame bitter. My favorite version of this is in preparation of collard greens. Alone and unbraised, collards are a harsh, leathery, bitter green. But throw some bacon in that pot and the sweetness of the collards cannot be tamed. Yes, throwing bacon in the pot will make everything taste better, but the saltiness of the bacon is also making the collards sweet and delicious. Salt suppresses bitter.

My dad used to eat grapefruits for breakfast. Gross, I know. He would just slice that mother in half and dig in with a fork. Who does this? Perhaps you have parents and grandparents who do this as well. Have you noticed that they generally have a trick up their sleeve for enjoying what is otherwise the most bitter of citrus fruits? They put salt on it. If you've never done this, let's #TeachYoMouth.

Try a grapefruit as it is, and then with salt. Suddenly the overwhelming bitter taste fades away and you're left with this rich, sweet citrus juice. This effect is key to food and wine pairing, because as you now know, oak is a bitter sensation in your wine. And how many of our wines are aged in oak? That's right, a *lot*. Making sure your meal, then, is well seasoned is important. Let's taste to see how this all really works.

Take a bite of that sweet strawberry, acclimate, swallow, and let it linger. Remember what happens when we drink the oaked red wine? Take a sip. The sweetness of the strawberry makes that red wine seem astringent and bitter, right? What if you put some salt on that same strawberry (I know, this is weird; just bear with me for a didactic exercise)? Sprinkle and take a bite. The first thing you will notice is that the strawberry might seem sweeter and more "strawberry-y" than ever. What's going on here?

Ever hear Tom Colicchio unload on a *Top Chef* contestant for *under-seasoning* a dish, for serving bland food? He asks them angrily, "Did you even taste the dish?" He harangues chefs when they don't put enough salt in their food because salt unlocks the flavor of food. This is partly why that strawberry will be tastier than ever before. This is also why you typically put a pinch of salt in your desserts: it unlocks flavors. It is also why dark chocolate with sea salt is so tasty: salt suppresses the bitter cocoa taste. Try that red wine again after your bite of salted strawberry. Is the wine different? Is it less astringent and less bitter than the sip after the bite of the strawberry that had no salt? Magic! That is the most important thing you as a wine lover can look for when pairing your food with oaky wines: make sure your food has enough salt! That salt will prevent your wine from falling apart, from turning into an abominable, harsh, desiccating punch to the mouth.

Now, let's be real, what restaurant in America isn't putting hefty pinches of salt on all their food? The truth is that salt is apparent in almost every dish, but be aware that the more oak in your wine, the more salt you should look for in your food. This is the essence of my love of oaky Chardonnay and salty potato chips.

This rule is perhaps the most important of the five. Finding dishes that are well seasoned will keep your wine intact and keep a perfectly delicious and oaky wine (O+) from disappointing you. If these are the wines you like, look for salty dishes, and enjoy without fear.

#TeachYoMouth Moment: Neutral Wines

Neutral is a potentially confusing and vague term; I apologize. Perhaps a better word to orient you is subtle. Think sushi and fresh seafood. Whether a California roll, a slice of fatty tuna, or oysters on the half shell, some foods you love because their flavors are fresh, delicate, and subtle. So this final rule is different. It is the only rule that seeks to prevent a rare occurrence: the wine corrupting the cuisine.

In one sense, this rule is the opposite of the previous #TeachYoMouth moment. Where the previous rule gives you salt for your oaky wines, this one gives you unoaked wines for non-salty foods. Let's take sushi as an example of how simple, fresh, and subtle can be corrupted easily. But wait, you say—salt can help you tame that oak in your Chardonnay or Cabernet, so why wouldn't the saltiness of soy sauce on your sushi tackle those oaky wines? Well it can, but the amount of soy sauce you'll likely need to slather on that mackerel would ruin the subtle, oily, rich fish you set out to eat. Instead, just stick with an unoaked wine like Chablis, Prosecco, Provençal Rose, Grüner Vetliner, or New Zealand Sauvignon Blanc (B-O-S-S+). Then there is no oak or bitterness to compete with the fresh, subtle flavors of the fish.

With delicate cuisines like sushi or lobster or oysters, be aware that many, many styles of wines will present a problem. In fact most of the wines you are drinking—a Barolo aged two years in oak, a mildly oaked white Burgundy, California Chardonnay, or even low-tannin red wine like low-cost California or Oregon Pinot Noir—present problems with this cuisine. Why? All of these wines will have at least some bitterness, if not significant bitterness, from their oak profile. Keep your wines low in oak if your food has subtle flavors.

Not all of us have access to delicious and fresh sushi and seafood year-round, so I'll ask that you #TeachYoMouth this lesson next time you pass through a restaurant that is up to the task. Conversely, if you have a reliable local purveyor or Whole Foods, try your oysters or unseasoned seafood with the Pinot Grigio and oaked red wine. You'll notice how the tannins and bitter flavors of the oaked red wine will provide some stiff competition to those delicate foods. The crisp Pinot Grigio, on the other hand, will make an excellent teammate, complementing the delicate, fresh flavors of the sea and allowing both food and wine to shine.

So in one short chapter and twenty minutes of eating and drinking, we've covered all the essentials of food and wine pairing. We've learned how the tastes in your wine interact with the tastes in your food. You now appreciate that nothing about food and wine pairing has to do with matching red meats with red wines, and white wines with fish and chicken. It comes down to how these dishes are prepared. If a big piece of mahi-mahi has a nice salted crust on it, have no fear ordering a big oaky

Barolo if that's what you love. If you're enjoying a steak, there is no reason why you can't still enjoy a glass of the Sancerre you love so much. Colors don't matter, nor do flavors; the BOSS tastes do.

You also now see that some things deserve each other and some things need help. Sweet, sour, and subtle foods need to find those traits prominent in the wines. Spicy foods need help from sweet wines, and oaked wines need salt to make for a pleasant combo.

Now the fun begins. Once you've accounted for these five rules, the natural complexities of wines have the opportunity to express themselves, based on the flavors in your food. The spectrum of flavors of wines and their interaction with the spectrum of flavors in your food are what create the truly infinite universe of possibilities.

Remember our mushroom pasta and earthy Oregon Pinot Noir (B-O+S-S+)? Let's revisit what we've learned so we can diagnose what will happen. How will this pairing be guaranteed to delight? The Pinot is oaked, dry, and sour. If my waiter says the dish is well seasoned or topped with Pecorino Romano (i.e., has the salt to cut through the oak) and doesn't have a sweet sauce, I like my chances with this wine. My wine won't be tainted by the tastes in the dish. Success!

You are now officially equipped to find God or hate yourself with food and wine pairing. *You have the rest of your life*

*to experiment, enjoy, and savor the wondrous food and wine bounty
that the world offers.*

They say happiness is found through the heart. I'm not so
sure. I find joy through my stomach. Whether it's butterflies
before a first date, or the punch to the gut when you are
dumped, you feel those things in your offal, which might be
why offal is so delicious. The joy I feel in my belly when it is
well fed with wine and food is a sensational yet fleeting taste of
the eternal, proof of God. Hallelujah.

CHAPTER 5

ADVANCED CONCEPTS

Are you suggesting coconuts migrate?
—Monty Python and the Holy Grail

Wine is 80 percent water and 12–15 percent alcohol; the rest consists of small components of tannin, nitrogen, and sulfites. The modest percentage of alcohol and the small percentage of everything else create all the nuances and the great many styles of wine; it's the difference between $15 Josh Cellars Cabernet Sauvignon, $125 Beringer Private Reserve

Cabernet Sauvignon, and $400 Chateau Haut-Brion, which is mostly Cabernet Sauvignon. The nerd in me can't help but draw a correlation with DNA. Humans share 90 percent of their DNA with fish, 98 percent with chimpanzees, and 99.9 percent with every other human being on the planet.[2] That last 0.1 percent creates Shaq, J. Lo, Peter Dinklage, and my mother. Such it is with wine; the minute differences in the wine's natural compounds create major differences in the wine you drink.

Throughout the book I've referenced some "advanced concepts," things that describe the subtleties of wine and things that make the truly great wines worthy of devotion, things like complexity, texture, length, structure, and longevity. You don't need to know these things; they won't make you a better lover, employee, or parent, but as you continue to drink more wine, practicing and tasting, you may grow to appreciate these qualities. I also don't want to let any wine shop turd-burglars use these words to intimidate you. Let's peel these fancy terms apart and make them less mysterious.

As we peel, appreciate that our units of measurement won't be anything as precise as microns or millimeters. We are likely to never achieve a scale that can measure length or texture like

2   Nancy Hopkins, "Falling in Love with DNA," Scientific American Frontiers website, Public Broadcasting Service, http://www.pbs.org/saf/1202/features/hopkins4.htm.

we can alcohol, residual sugar, or acid. Think horseshoes and hand grenades: close is good enough.

Complexity: Not That Complex

Complexity is the simplest notion of all the advanced concepts and generally the first thing even the most untrained palate notices when drinking wine. For the same reason that adding salt, then pepper, then béarnaise sauce can increase your delight of a simple cut of beef, the more flavors in a wine, the more likely your enjoyment. This is what complexity is about. Our mouths notice this increasing complexity. With practice, which will start momentarily, you will be able to discern this objectively.

This is also where the ridiculous tasting notes come from, those little flowery poems of flavors from the ridiculous wine writers. The more flavors apparent—from fruity to savory, floral to vegetal, earthy to spicy—the more complex you could interpret the wine to be. This is the only reason why tasting notes can be worthwhile. When done with integrity, they suggest a level of complexity in a wine. But it seems all wineries create exotic, complex tasting notes to make the wine sound as appealing as possible, no matter the wine's true complexity. This does not help you. But as you taste more wine, you will notice different levels of complexity across wines, without any help from a tasting note. With time, you will be able to start labeling the flavors you taste yourself!

If you're keeping me honest, there are two challenges to our understanding of complexity that potentially confuse this otherwise simple notion: one, people have different sensitivities to different tastes, and two, as we've discussed, most of what you taste you are actually smelling. When you have a peppercorn-encrusted steak, you will say it tastes delicious and nobody will bust your balls to remind you that you're technically smelling the peppercorns. If someone does point that out, they are likely to make dinner horribly insufferable. We can all simply agree that the steak tastes good even though you're smelling the pepper.

Also, taste is personal. Just because something is more complicated doesn't mean you need to like it. But, no matter your taste, a roomful of people can arrive at an objective conclusion on whether something is complex. But enough talk; let's taste an example, starting with the much-maligned Pinot Grigio.

#TeachYoMouth Moment: Complexity

Many people in this world love Pinot Grigio because it's easy-drinking, crisp, and refreshing. The criticism is usually that the wine is boring, simple, or even bland when compared to other white wines. The bad rap mostly comes from peoples' critique of Santa Margherita Pinot Grigio (B-O-S-S+), which is dollar for dollar, perhaps the single blandest wine on this planet. I'm not saying it's bland, but at $20+ a bottle, boy are you missing out. Santa Margherita is a mass-production wine that seeks a consistent product, not necessarily a wine that paints a picture of a distinct land or vintage conditions and shows you true character (remember terr-WAH?). You might notice hints of citrus, green apples, and grass when you taste this wine. Compare that to a Pinot Grigio made by someone whose family has been making wine for seven centuries and now growing grapes on the rugged slopes of Alto Adige outside Trentino. Giovanni Bonmartini-Fini's Barone Fini Pinot Grigio (B-O-S-S+) comes from a sustainable farming enterprise that existed long before "sustainable farming" became a popular modern concept. While these two Pinot Grigios have the exact same BOSS profile, my bet is that nine out of ten people will prefer the Barone Fini because of its greater complexity. As you smell it, you will notice a range of citrus and floral aromas, like lemon zest, honeysuckle, and white flower petals. You'll taste flavors of fresh red apples, juicy white peaches, lemons, and lime. This is a perfect case study of complexity. There is, quite simply, more going on in the Barone Fini Pinot Grigio.

Having said that, we are all different. Some people prefer a latte, some people a cappuccino. Some people prefer a white sauce with pasta, some a red. And some completely insane people prefer Pepsi over Coke, which I will never understand. Our natural genetic makeup, our experiences with food and drink, and our evolution of tastes all play a role in what we like.

So someone could legitimately prefer a less complex wine. The sum experience of the wine doesn't define better or worse, just different. But one cannot deny a fundamental difference in the complexity. Taste these two Pinot Grigio wines and you will come to appreciate that.

Length Matters

Length is an easily grasped concept, although you may not be paying attention to it. Length refers to how long the flavors of a wine linger in your mouth, something not generally appreciated by the common drinker. Many wines are fun at the outset, full of fruity goodness and rich complexity, and then suddenly, the flavors evaporate. These wines exploit our ability to be distracted and only offer flavor complexity at the onset—that is, they show very little length. This is something early students of wine won't notice or think to notice, but it's such a defining feature of the truly great wines: they go on and on and on …. Consider tasting a spoonful of plain white rice and a spoonful of molasses: won't they have extraordinarily different lengths? Similarly, really nice wines outlast their simpler counterparts in overwhelming fashion.

Texture's My Favorite

Texture is something much overlooked even by seasoned palates, but something to which I'm personally particularly sensitive.

To me, a wine can't be great without great texture. Cheap, ill-made wines can often deliver an offensive textural experience. Merlot and Syrah are often blended into red wines in small quantities so that they can create a more pleasant texture in your mouth, not to mention the added complexity that comes from the flavors of additional grapes. One of my favorite winemakers when it comes to texture is Zach Long from Kunde Family Estate, a winemaker respectful of tradition but willing to push boundaries, in addition to being very intelligent and knowledgeable. I swear I learn something new every time I talk to Zach.

Zach coaxes great texture from his wines and is masterful in blending nontraditional grapes in a wine to achieve that great texture. He adds Viognier to the Kunde Family's Sauvignon Blanc, which adds the layer of flavors unique to the Viognier grape, but also makes the Sauvignon Blanc softer and more luxurious. While this would not be allowed in French Sauvignon Blanc-growing regions like Sancerre and Bordeaux (the French government closely regulates what grapes are used in which regions), it is very much inspired by the French sensibility for texture. This is one of the major reasons why Semillon is blended with Sauvignon Blanc in the white wines of Bordeaux. The Semillon not only adds new flavors and a nutty complexity, it creates softer texture and heavier weight in the wine.

The best wines are soft and viscous, or even velvety and luxurious. Quite simply, other wines are not. In time, you will come to appreciate that wines can fall anywhere on this texture spectrum. Truth be told, a wine can't be great just because it has great texture, but it can set a wine apart from the pack.

Structure Deconstructed

Okay, now it's going to get a little complicated. Let's discuss structure. Once again, it's probably more complicated than it needs to be, but this time it's been made complicated because everyone seems to have their own version of what structure means. In fairness, with structure, the individual didactic concepts that we've isolated in the previous pages are convoluted as we seek to articulate a convergence of individual factors, only experienced in your mouth. So it can get confusing.

No matter the expert, all would agree that structure is not one trait, but a combination of characteristics. Structure is the sum physiological experience of a wine in your mouth, excluding the flavors. Since most of the flavors you experience are actually smells, you can limit structure to what you taste and "feel," versus what you smell.

Simply broken down to cause and effect, structure is the combination of tannin, acid, alcohol, and sugar in your wine that creates a mix of body, bitter (oak), sweet, and sour, apparent from the first taste on the tip of your tongue, to the full mouth-coating experience of a big gulp, down to the final taste left in your mouth after you've swallowed the wine. Most of structure is a textural experience, and as I mentioned before, texture is a hard thing to observe for a new wine drinker. Look for four things when learning to assess structure:

Does acid create a raciness and zippiness in the wine, or not?

Do the oak and tannin create dryness, or not? Are they overbearing or well integrated into the wine?

Is the texture soft and plush, or sharp and angular?

Does it have big body and weight, or not?

The sum experience of these components reflects its structure. A wine with good structure will have all of these elements in balance. A wine without structure or with poor structure will be missing one or more of the critical components or one element will be out of balance. For example, when there is a lack of acid or tannin, or if the texture or weight doesn't seem to fit with the level of acid or tannin, these are wines that have shortcomings in their structure. If the wine has really high alcohol and a big body, but low acid and tannin, you could argue the wine is out of balance or has poor structure. You might even hear people get more specific about structure, describing acid structure or tannin structure, but those subsets of the wine's overall structure only refer to the apparent presence of acid or tannin in the wine and what they contribute.

When people talk about structure, they are diagnosing the sum experience of the wine. They are assessing how each of these four factors integrates into a wine. Understanding structure, then, takes lots of practice. We discussed at the outset of the book how learning wine is like learning a foreign language. After you master the vocabulary, you have to learn how to apply the vocabulary in a variety of life circumstances. Similarly, understanding how structure can vary from wine to wine requires familiarity with the vast range of wines and the different circumstances they present you in a glass.

For the true beginners out there, you are not likely to master the concept of structure immediately. Come back to this section often as you continue to taste more wines. Because while these subtle components will take time and practice to observe and describe, structure is ultimately what sets the truly great wines apart from the rest.

Wait a tick, why again do we care about structure? More than anything, structure dictates the potential longevity of a wine. Fortunately, longevity isn't a prerequisite for enjoying the wine you're having with dinner tonight, on your next date night, or along with your next Netflix binge. It is a unique trait needed for collectible and rare wines. If you're not collecting rare wines, feel free to ignore this next section.

The Rarity of Longevity

Longevity is another challenging concept. One confusing input, structure, creates one confusing output, longevity. You recall my perverted observations on drinking old wines, and how it really is a rare group of wines that can successfully achieve longevity. These wines are made long-lived primarily because of the intense oak regimen the wines see. This attention to structure requires an expensive oak regimen that only rare grapes can endure successfully and in which few wineries elect to invest. The tannin imparted from a lengthy period in oak barrels protects the wine throughout its life and evolution. Without the oak's tannin, the wine will lose its fruit flavors, and other funkier flavors will emerge.

Equally important, a wine with adequate acid will ensure that the fruit and complexity of the wine maintain their intensity over time. Wines without this acid will lose that fresh fruit flavor, devolving quickly into tired, dusty, earthier wines. This is most of my experience with drinking older California wines. There are of course many, many exceptions to this in California, but recall what the tendencies of California wine are: more alcohol and lower acid (B+OSS-). This is why you see people drinking more old European wine than you do old American wine. You could argue that this isn't a shortcoming in American wine, but simply what Americans want. You could argue that producers would change and adapt their product to be more like Europeans, if that's what Americans wanted. And you'd be right. Whether it's the native winemaking environment, the preferences of consumers, or both, you end up with the same result: American wines aren't nearly as long-lived as their European counterparts, due in no small part to the inadequate acid in their structure.

CHAPTER 6

STORY TIME

That's what optimistic means, you know? It means stupid. An optimist is somebody who goes, "Hey, maybe something nice will happen." Why the f*** would anything nice happen?
—**Louis C.K.,** from *Hilarious*, 2011

For better and for worse, the wine business is unlike any other business. It is irrational, entrenched in the past, and jam-packed with old white men, not unlike Congress.

It is also romantic, enriching, and immensely satisfying, not unlike wine itself. If you permit me to reach, the wine business is an outstanding metaphor for the human experience, capable of painful failures and frustrations, but also of monumental successes and spectacular, joyous achievements. Its pain and glory are intertwined, as artists and the bottom line seem to act out the same doomed Shakespearean play, where economic busts and booms expose ineptitude and naïveté but also give rise to new pioneers and resurrect fortunes of once-forgotten glories. Told you I was gonna reach.

My plan with this chapter was to give you a brief peek behind the curtain of the wine business, showing you some of the beauty and the beast. The revelation, of course, wouldn't be the beauty, as it is readily apparent. If you see me driving through the vineyards of Calistoga for a winery meeting on a Tuesday afternoon, tasting through a flight of small production Russian River Pinot Noir at eleven o'clock in the morning on a Thursday, sneaking in and out of tastings from the iconic producers at *Wine Spectator's* Wine Experience another day, or at a dinner with a winemaker and his wines paired by a talented chef, you might think, wow, this is a sweet gig. And most days, it is a very good gig.

But the beast lurks; the business has a rarely exposed underbelly. In stark contrast to its apparent perks, it is a frustrating line of work, it's a tough business, and it's remarkably unglamorous before and after those tastings and winemaker dinners. If it wasn't a tough business, Warren Buffett would have found us years ago. It is famously said in the wine business that if you want to make $1 million, start out with ten. So many wineries over the years have started in the upswing of economic cycles, with people passionately devoted to the business and eager to invest in a fancy new winery and tasting room. Not long after, hard times hit, and the inventory that took them many years to prepare is now unsalable.

My plan was to share some of the many failures that the larger wine companies seem to make routine and some of the heartbreaking personal stories of good people that could not overcome hardship. My plan was to give you an unadulterated view of how tough the business is.

My editor called this chapter a "bit of a downer." After I stopped laughing, I realized she was right. I also realized I was in danger of becoming the Perez Hilton of wine, and none of the fine (and perhaps the not-so-fine) people actually deserve a push in front of the bus. So I committed to only sharing the fun, uplifting stories. If you are disappointed or really curious, I can be bribed with Premier Cru Chablis.

We're Adorable

As an industry, we are adorably uncompetitive. There's no dumpster-diving to uncover and tape together competitive trade secrets from shredded documents. There's no lobbying to change FDA regulations, no falsifying of documents, no poison pill strategies, no attack campaigns. You could even argue that we should be more ruthless, but we are not.

I think you can attribute this pacifism to one of two things, perhaps a mix of both. Robert Mondavi believed in the 1970s that to be successful, we had to work together. At that time, we weren't competing with each other as much as we were competing with the belief that California wine wasn't capable of world-class quality. While that shared challenge no longer exists, you still see this same camaraderie throughout the industry today. When wine tasting in Napa and Sonoma, I know this is the case. Most of the people working in the vineyards, cellars, and tasting rooms have traded jobs across multiple wineries. They get off work and they hang out with each other, swapping wines and sharing their favorites at barbecues and parties. There is a sense of community, family, and friendship that assumes we can all succeed doing what we all do best, especially as different as we all do it. I say mostly because it can get downright catty when winemaker or industry executive egos are involved, and oh, are there a few fragile egos. But mostly, there is shared passion and genuine appreciation for others' successes. Ultimately, I think this community of wine lovers genuinely relishes in the great myriad of wines that are made distinct by different people and different lands. It is a mutual appreciation of the beverage itself that underlies the fraternity.

The other possible source of this pacifism is less romantic and probably more accurate, but it only holds true for wines over $10. For these wines, the success of any one winery is less about what a competitor does and more about controlling the circumstances under which your own wine gets to market. If Crest releases a new tartar-prevention toothpaste, you can bet Colgate will follow. If Charmin decreases its price $0.50 per four-roll pack, Cottonelle will respond. Conversely, if Opus One decreases its price by $5 per bottle, it won't have any effect on how much wine Schafer or Caymus sell or how they sell it. If a winery wants to sell more wine, it plans with its distributors the outlets, investments, and marketing activity required to do so. The clout or influence to push a distributor or retailer to change the potential of a brand through distribution, promotion, and merchandising is the defining feature of its growth potential, not competition.

In addition to being adorably uncompetitive, we are also adorably irrational. One of my favorite stories is how there came to be two Stags Leaps wineries in Napa Valley. Most people don't know that there are two wineries that bear almost the exact same name. Most, in fact, are confused if a Stags' Leap Winery Cabernet arrives at the table when they are expecting a Stag's Leap Wine Cellars Cabernet. Just as you might have noticed the different placement of the apostrophe on "Stags" in the previous sentence, they might notice that the label they are used to seeing from their preferred Cabernet is apparently now subtly different. Why these almost imperceptible differences, and why is it so confusing?

For many, myself included, the Stags Leap District is hallowed ground, where the fading light of daily sunsets bounces off the jagged cliffs of this remote, hidden valley, creating prismatic mosaics of light against earth and vine. It is where pioneer Warren Winiarski first planted Cabernet grapes in 1970. Today, Napa is rich with posh hotels, spas, and world-class restaurants, an escape to a slower pace and the pinnacle of food and wine luxury. When Warren arrived, there was no guarantee the land would produce wine of any substance; there was only hope, and a lot of farming. He certainly didn't expect that the wines he made from this hallowed land, his second vintage in fact, would forever change the landscape of American wine. His 1973 Stag's Leap Wine Cellars Cabernet, along with wines from other Napa pioneers, would be submitted by Parisian wine merchant Steven Spurrier to a panel of French judges in a blind competition in Paris, a competition witnessed by a *Time* magazine journalist. The now famous "Judgment of Paris" in 1976, and the resulting cover of *Time* celebrating a victory of Americans over the greatest French wines, forever elevated Napa Valley's trajectory. Napa Valley Cabernet is now one of the elite wines of the world, and Warren and the Stags Leap district are inextricably linked to Napa's past and future.

Did I mention there was another winery down the road also bearing the Stags Leap name? Situated in a beautiful, historic stone mansion no less than a mile and a half down Silverado Trail from Stag's Leap Wine Cellars, this fraternal twin sources grapes from vineyards that bump into its twin and, in its own right, has a rich history and a winemaking pedigree that's head and shoulders above most in California. In fact, grapes have been grown on this beautiful property since the 1880s, well before the winemaking renaissance of the 1970s. The mansion, winery, and vineyard land were purchased and restored by Carl Doumani in 1971, and the wines have continued to set the bar for Stags Leap red wines over the years. Long story short, there have long been two Stags Leaps, and one decided to sue the other for the Stags Leap trademark.

A wise and just judge in Napa could not decide which of these two sparring siblings had a greater claim to the name. Where King Solomon threatened to slice a baby in half to decide who should win the prize, this sage hillbilly judge decided to carve up the baby, slice by slice. In 1986, it was forever decreed that Carl Doumani's Stags Leap would be called "Winery," it would have to put the apostrophe on the right side of the "s," and it had to maintain a leaping stag on its label. Warren's Stags Leap would be called "Stag's Leap Wine Cellars," and the accord dictated that its stag would have to be standing still. Huzzah! Totally different labels now! No more confusion! Right?

Could you imagine a judge deciding that Microsoft could sell a smartphone called "i'Phone" and bearing an apple logo but with a bite out of the left side instead of the right? Well, these two wineries, battling over a valuable brand name, something that consumers trust to find the wine they love, accepted a preposterous agreement that forced them to share the trademark under ridiculous conditions that are, in practice, imperceptible to most people. Only in Napa. We're adorable.

As silly as this case study is, something spectacular did emerge from the absurdity: a wine. The two warring factions relented under the terms set by the enlightened judge, and peace again reigned on this storied two-mile stretch of Silverado Trail. In honor of the agreement, the two wineries joined forces to release a 1985 Cabernet Sauvignon, called "The Accord," with 50 percent of the grapes coming from each estate's vines. A rarity never since repeated, I think, a couple bottles of this limited production wine were opened at a winery Christmas party in 2009, held in Doumani's restored stone mansion.

It was a fantastic wine. It was a fantastic Christmas party. Sipping a taste of this rare wine in a beautiful mansion as the sun spent its last breath on the stained-glass window in the dining room, which bears the words *ne cede malis*, or "don't give in to misfortune," words that defined the spirit of Napa's great pioneers, was one of those rare experiences in wine that won't ever let go of me. My hope is that you, too, have similar moments seared into your psyche, experiences with wine that won't let go of you. No amount of economic down cycles, vineyard pests, or bad vintages can temper these cherished experiences.

But wineries still fail and great wines can falter, as costs are cut or poor decisions are made by owners.

Perhaps eight years ago, I recall seeing a video of Venice's St. Mark's Square underwater. I was eighteen when I first visited Venice. I took a gondola ride through the canals with a singing Venetian at the helm, I fed the swarming pigeons in the center of the exquisitely paved square, and I reveled in the otherworldly beauty of this almost magical, floating city. Remember, I'm from Ohio; seeing Venice for the first time was *magic*. To see the square underwater and the city sinking many years later broke my heart. How could one of Italy's greatest treasures, a symbol of its dominance in trade, art, and architecture from long ago, begin to sink to the ocean floor like Atlantis?

Fortunately, PBS and a NOVA documentary restored my faith in the human experience. It turns out that since its inception Venice has been a massive public works project. Beneath the foundation of a nine-hundred-year-old cathedral in Torcello, just six miles northeast of St. Mark's Square by ferry, archaeologists uncovered evidence of several layers of ground built up around the foundation. It seems anything built on the marshes of Venice would inevitably sink to the bottom of the sea. So for centuries—dating back to the Romans in AD 200—a great many structures built on feeble marshland were either repeatedly raised at their foundations or were torn down and completely rebuilt. So it was in Torcello, where perhaps six individual adjustments to the foundation were made—sometimes raising the foundation six inches, sometimes a foot—and where they found the first proof that the seemingly magical city of Venice has always been a Big Dig. The sinking city wasn't doomed, it simply needed fresh repairs. What's amazing to me is that the human interventions made centuries ago were so effective that nobody in our time even knew they'd been made. Oddly, this gave me hope. It gave me hope that human ingenuity can overcome seemingly monumental challenges, and in some cases, that ingenuity is essential. So powerful can that ingenuity be, it even allows us to forget it for centuries.

Whenever I see a winery that I love shutter its doors or witness wonderful wines denigrated as hard times or mismanagement corrode the winery, I remind myself of the power of human ingenuity.

The American Dream

One of my favorite people in the wine business is Joseph Carr. His story embodies what I love about wine, the business, and the people. Joseph was born in a small hamlet in upstate New

York to a family that often had a hard time making ends meet, about as far away from Bordeaux or Napa as you could get. Joseph went to college, the first in his family. He took a job as a busboy at a local restaurant to help make ends meet. After his first week of work at the Big Tree Inn in Geneseo, New York, the owner sat him down and broke some news: "You are the worst busboy I've ever had." He gave Joseph a wine opener, a bow tie, and a book about wine, and told him that if he could learn to wield all three, he could be the wine steward. From his college bunk bed, he is suddenly traveling to Burgundy, Bordeaux, and Piedmont as he devoured the book. The wine business had its hooks in Joseph. He soon was in charge of wine lists at upscale restaurants in New York and Miami, and eventually worked his way into the business as a salesman, marketer, and ultimately an executive in Napa.

One day in 2002, after years battling in boardrooms, managing the bottom line, and making the best of the wine business, he was burned out. The daily grind of this challenging business had taken its toll. He opened a bottle of wine with his wife and started talking about what the next chapter held. They started talking about the American Dream and what it meant to him.

Remember the American Dream? The pure, non-cynical notion that if you dreamed big and worked hard you could make a better life for yourself? Joseph is a believer in it. To him, no matter what economic or political turmoil we've witnessed in our country, it has never faded, rusted, or hid from sight. It's a real thing, and after the second bottle of wine, he decided that he had to pursue his. He took out a second mortgage on his house and went back to Napa, but this time to make wine. He slept on couches, trained alongside Freemark Abbey winemaker, Ted Edwards, and learned to make wine. In 2005, he released his first vintage of Joseph Carr Cabernet Sauvignon, the wine that is to this day the house wine at the Big Tree Inn.

Meet Joseph Carr today and you are tempted to think it was an easy journey. He has a sparkling smile, he can't work for more than twenty minutes without poking fun at himself, and more than anything, he loves to share his wine with people. Every time I hear him tell his story, I get goose bumps. I get angry when he leaves a part of the story out and I get angrier when he tells a part I have never heard before. What you don't see in Joseph is the frustration of a bad vintage when you're putting your life savings into a wine, the long days on the road, selling wine out of the back of your car to people who have never heard of you, and the financial strain of burying a mountain of cash into assets that you can't sell for at least a year. Joseph doesn't dwell on that; he would rather tell you about the people he has met along the way, the retailers who sold his first vintage of wine when he was unknown, the Larson family who helped him source, blend, and bottle his first wines, and the couple who shared a bottle of Joseph Carr Cabernet on their first date, only to serve it at their wedding three years later.

Now, I'd be the first to admit that I wouldn't be waxing poetic if he made awful wine. But on top of all his charm and his uplifting story, he still makes great wine. I can't help but root for this guy.

Cheering Section

A sommelier at hot spot in New York City said to me, "We'll carry Veuve, but you're going to pay for it." Veuve Clicquot is a storied Champagne brand, made legendary by one of the first wine entrepreneurs—not to mention one of the first triumphant female entrepreneurs in early nineteenth-century France, a time when women weren't supposed to be business visionaries. This historic Champagne house crafts wonderful vintage wines but also churns out mass quantities of a yellow label, non-vintage Champagne that retails for about $50. Vintage Champagne is only made in great years; non-vintage Champagne is made every year and is a blend of multiple years' worth of wine. If you like bubbles at brunch, Veuve will scratch the itch. Does it encapsulate all the splendor and magnificence that a grower Champagne does, wine made from vineyard land lovingly cultivated by local families for centuries? Or is it a blend of hundreds of acres of vineyards, fermented in vats the size of houses, meant to drive out a consistent product year after year, not unlike a can of Budweiser? "I've got a dozen grower Champagnes that are superior and cheaper, but because you don't want to use my expertise and instead drink a brand no different than your Gucci loafers and Mercedes S Class, I'm marking that Veuve up 300 percent, and everyone's happy."

The sommelier at this hot spot has imposed a cowardice tax. He will charge obscene prices for Veuve because he would much rather you ask about a lower-priced, grower Champagne made by a family that has worked their land for generations and painstakingly kept the business afloat through economic recessions, hail, *phylloxera*, and the socialist impositions of a highly regulated French wine business. You will root for these wines if you get to know them, and I'd be willing to bet that if you tasted his grower Champagne against Veuve, you'd pick his recommendation every time.

Earlier in my career, I once asked Jeff Kunde of Kunde Family Estate what he likes to drink. I was an eager, ambitious student, hungry to make personal connections with the people who made wine in California. When he's out at a restaurant, what was his favorite wine? I was expecting an esoteric answer, a small production Roussanne from the Sonoma Coast, premier cru Chablis, or something perhaps I hadn't heard of. If you know how country Jeff is, you would know that any of those answers would be preposterous. Jeff is a better hunter than Champagne drinker, unless it's the champagne of beers. I was at first disappointed with how boring his answer was. He said, "If I don't see a Kunde wine, I try to find one of my friends' wines."

While I still geek out on rare or esoteric wines with the best of them, I now appreciate Jeff's answer. Anything old from the Loire generally excites me, as do grower Champagnes, the dry wines of Portugal, and Chardonnay from the Sonoma Coast. But when I order wine now, I look for friends. I look for the wines made by people I love, made with love I know they've given. I don't so much order a wine as I do root for a friend. There really is so much great wine out there; sometimes it's hard to go wrong. I say this of course having spent the past eight years in San Francisco and Manhattan, where the great wine spoils of the world are readily available—so I'm a bit of a spoiled brat. When I go home to Cincinnati, it can be a bit more challenging to find those rare gems lovingly sought out by sommeliers, wine shop owners, and restaurants, but even the big, nationally distributed wine brands are regularly worth their money, especially if you know what you're looking for.

Fortunately, you are now a BOSS, so you know what you're looking for. You are also equipped to try new wines without fear of failure or intimidation. You are free to find your own wine moments, where you root for your friends and the wines you love, and where, despite what Louis C.K. says, nice things happen regularly.

EPILOGUE
BE A BOSS

Go into all the world and preach the good news to everyone.
—Jesus

O ver the years I've seen many restaurants brilliantly rise from the pack to present wine in straightforward, helpful ways. Shout-out to Motorino, my preferred delivery and dine-in pizza joint in New York City: they happen to encapsulate all that I want wine education to be about. This wonderful little East Village prize does 100 percent of what is needed with their simple but high-quality wine list, seemingly as instinctively as they prepare simple but high-quality cuisine. With their blessing, I'm including a grainy picture from my old iPhone that illustrates how helpful their wine list is.

Do you see this simple, accurate approach to describing wines? While hopefully we've taken it a step further in this book, let's be honest; this is *more* than adequate when you're actually at this restaurant to catch up with an old friend or attend to your date. Most days, this is as much time as most people want to spend thinking about wine. Seriously, Motorino, *thank you* for giving people the simple information they need to make a decision.

Another shout-out to my favorite wine bar, Terroir in New York City: the benchmark against which all other wine experiences should be measured. They don't just offer you wine; they don't just offer you the standard facts of sourcing, vintage, and winemaking techniques for those who are curious; they offer you philosophy, history, politics, morality, and religion. They want you to understand the diversity of wine, and they want you to appreciate its context, either via historical events or winemaking tradition. Their wine list is more manifesto than menu. From the "Summer of Riesling," to their celebration of Liebfraumilch, sherry, port, and Madeira, to their daily commitment to showcasing all the forgotten, overlooked, or underestimated redheaded orphans in the world of wine, these guys are truly doing the Lord's work, and I am a faithful disciple. Wine is a human endeavor with beauty and tragedy, triumph and failure, delight and devastation, and the brilliant philosophers and hedonists at Terroir champion and protect this culture. If that feels like overkill for a night out, then simply revel in the fact that they have perhaps the greatest selections of wines available by the glass in the entire country, and somehow the entire staff knows almost everything about each wine. This place is primed for you to experiment happily and with success. (And they make these tasty blue cheese and beet arancini, a must-have with a Savennières.)

Our country is filled with food and wine Oprahs, people willing to grant your belly their favorite things. While traveling, I dined alone one night at the bar of Michael Mina in San Francisco, where I met a young sommelier, Evan Hufford, a guy who would bring out the food and wine nut in all of us. In my standard high-maintenance fashion, I started asking questions about the bitters they use in their Manhattans, what vermouths the bartenders prefer, and did I order the right appetizer? Rather than be annoyed with my peppering of self-serving questions, he started pouring. He poured for me the two vermouths he liked, then a rye and bourbon whisky side by side to showcase everything that makes for the best Manhattan. And when my food came, he poured a half-dozen wines for me to gauge how well each paired with my three-course meal. I had more glassware than the table of six behind me. For no other reason than my curiosity, this guy opened his bar and cellar to me so that I would not only hear his answers, but understand his answers. With places like Motorino, Terroir, Michael Mina, and thousands more like them across the country, you have almost infinite resources to shape your understanding of wine.

And while knowledge, information, and understanding are all great, there is one thing more important than all of it. I can explain all of these basic or advanced concepts to death, you can master them, you can plot out a BOSS profile for every wine on this planet. But ultimately something very simple can overrule logic as you pursue a path to consistent pleasure with wine.

A friend was telling me about a couple who spent their honeymoon in Italy, and being the oenophiles that they are, they drank loads of wine and ate loads of great food. In a small town along the coast, outside Rome, they fell in love with a magnificent wine. That's not, of course, how they started telling the story. They first recounted the story by describing the warmth of the owner's grandmother, the vista over the sapphire-blue Mediterranean Sea from the intricately laid patio cut into the jagged cliffs, the freshness of the seafood and the handmade pasta, and, of course, the outstanding wine the owner's family has been making for centuries in this small fishing town. They insisted that the owner sell them a case of the magical wine, and they brought it home. The lone solace of the return flight back to the States after such a trip was the wine they could treasure for years to come. Many months later, they opened a bottle for the wife's birthday. To their chagrin, it just wasn't the same. Had they been duped? They couldn't believe that sweet old lady would have switched out the wine they adored for a lesser wine. What happened to the wine; was it the flight back? Was it stored improperly?

Most likely, the wine hadn't changed. What was missing was the magic of the experience. The personal connections, the glorious settings, and rich cultures we enjoy while drinking wine inevitably dial up our delight. There's nothing wrong with that couple's initial conclusions; their original joy is no less valid than any other experience, but it was the sensory overload of the entire experience that defined their perception of the wine. Back home, there was no vista, no grandmother, no seafood fresh from the Mediterranean—all of the things that had made them root for the wine. And those experiences will trump everything else that you can touch, taste, or smell. And frankly, that's why most of us love wine: the experience of sharing it with special people in special moments. Or sharing it with myself on my couch watching "Freestyle Fridays" on *106 and Park*. I highly recommend Sicilian wines for these gangsta moments.

My guess is that you can recount a similar experience, if not many experiences, where you felt like the center of the wine universe, where the wine gods saw fit to bestow upon you a singularly divine wine drinking experience that could never be replicated. If not, get out there and find yours. If so, go find more.

It was only eight years ago that I started reading *Wine for Dummies* when the only difference I could spy between wines was their color. I had no discernible gifts in learning about wine and no innate advantage in articulating what I tasted. If anything, I was naturally worse at wine tasting than others with equally minimal training. Bottom line, if I can I learn wine, so can you.

If you're spending less than $10 on wine, stand and be counted. Don't be ashamed, and don't let anyone give you crap for drinking affordable wines. In fact, I hereby grant you permission to enjoy the wines you enjoy without fear of reprisal or snob judgment. No different than enjoying your favorite pizza, burger, or coffee, you should feel empowered to drink all that the wine world offers and select only the ones you love.

That said, I'd be willing to wager that, over time, those of you who are new wine drinkers or who only prefer sweet wines will eventually gravitate to drier wines, as most people do. Most people don't enjoy their first taste of black coffee, and start by adding lots of milk and sugar. That evolution is no different than your trajectory with wine; your tastes will evolve the more you drink. Enjoy that journey. Neither you nor I liked broccoli when we were children. When I was in college, I did not like sushi. Three years ago, I would push the tripe in my Vietnamese pho to the side and leave it in the bowl. Now all of these things I eat lovingly.

Similarly, when I started in wine, I adored Aussie Shiraz and Côtes du Rhône and didn't like dessert wines at all. While I still enjoy and appreciate Shiraz and Côtes du Rhône, I now drink two times as much white wine as I do red, and you can't keep my grubby paws away from Sauternes and other dessert wines. Learning a construct to understand wine will help you now, of course, but it will also help you explore and appreciate new wines over time, assimilating the great diversity of the wines into your palate as time goes on.

Now that you understand how wines can be grouped together given their stylistic similarities, like a BOSS, the traditional wine education books are terrific at explaining why. They will go into the varietal, *terroir*, and winemaking differences that create vastly different wine traditions and final wines in your glass. Enjoy these books, now that you've learned the basic vocabulary to describe all of the world's wines, as these talented authors take you deep into the wine regions of the world.

It is a sincere pleasure for me to bring people into this world. My sisters (yay! you made the book, Jacqueline!) for so long would only drink Sauvignon Blanc from New Zealand. Over time, I converted them to white Bordeaux, Sancerre, Chardonnays from California, and even Muscadet. Now, admittedly, they still shame me by putting ice in their wine from time to time, but I'm honestly happy that they are enjoying wine on their terms, and they aren't afraid to explore, ask questions, and find new things to try. That is my greatest hope with this book: that it will expand your options and create a better wine adventure for you. Please find me on Twitter, Instagram, or Facebook to keep the conversation going. Until I sell some books, I expect most of the dialogue will be with my mother, but all are welcome.

My other hope is that there will be a time when you come to like or at least appreciate all of the wines we've discussed in the book. While I certainly have my favorite wines, it is the occasion or food that force my wine decisions more than my natural preferences or aversions to sweetness or tannin or acid. When summer hits, the flavors and freshness of mussels and Muscadet are best to beat the summer heat. Chablis and sushi, an adventure in texture as much as flavor, is an all-time favorite, with rich, velvety, and crisp Chablis perfectly suited to rich, velvety, and fatty tuna. Fried chicken and Beaujolais, forget about it. Port and smoky barbecue, Savennières and funky blue cheese, salty potato chips and Napa Valley Chardonnay, roasted chicken and rosé, right-bank Bordeaux and aged beef, and Sauternes milkshakes—how great is life?

Let's go spread some gospel.

#LearnByDrinking

#TeachYoMouth

ACKNOWLEDGMENTS

Thanks to my Mom and Dad, Jennifer, Jacqueline, Cam, Grandma and Grandpa Schehl, Grandma Schiller and Superpops, Kathy and Jerry, Mike and Mary Jo, Bob and Kelly, Patti and Barney, Barbie, Tom and Janie, and each of my cousins.

Elliott, Cole and Oliver, you can take no credit but I love you no less.

Thank you to my friends that are family: Amber Balestrieri, Brent and Jill Dalke, Peggy Gsell, Danny and Jenny Heisel, Andrew Iappini, Mark Krieg, Catherine Marquette, Kevin and Laura Murray, Dave Pan, Doug Langway, Ross and Lauren

Levine, Jonathan Lehr, Jack and Julia Nicolson, Katie Smithson, Jin Ho "Bob" Park, Stinson Parks, John and Annie Taglianetti, Carla Vaccarezza, Sophie and David Vasquez, Kevin and Susie Wojcikewych, and Jeff Wuorinen.

Thank you to my many teachers over the years: Mike Aitken, Tony Austin, Bonnie Barest, Elizabeth Barrutia, Steve Black, Lynne Bartron, Giovanni Bonmartini-Fini, Mike Burns, Adam Chase, Joseph Carr, Nicole Carter, Leticia Chacon-Rodriguez, Jerry Comfort, Jeff Corbett, Keith Duncan, John Drady, Jorge de Castro, Pieter de Graaf, Bill Deutsch, Peter Deutsch, Marco DiGiulio, Wayne Donaldson, Kasra Ferdows, Matt Foley, Sean Gibson, Bill Hahn, Kristine Hankinson, Francoise Hanonik, Jorge Hernandez, Laurie Hook, Elizabeth Hooker, Rob Jensen, Zach Long, Suzy Kilgore, Jeff Kunde, Kevin McKenna, Michael Murphy, Aaron Pott, Bill Piersol, Phil Pyrce, Renato Reyes, Pat Roney, Ryan Rowder, Lori Rubinson, Mark Salmon, Francesca Schuler, Tom Smallhorn, Kelly Soendker, Peter Szemenyei, Tom Steffanci, Dave Trebilcock, Anthony Van Nice, Teal Williams, Peter Willmert, and Joe Wiza.

Thank you for the friendship and support of those that I have the privilege of working with, no matter how infrequent: Kim Ahearn, Lisa Browne, Rebecca Canan, Carrie Reed, Cathy Dangler, Peggy Gsell, Chris Hayes, Isaac Herrera, Ashley

Mayhew Jenkins, Meghan Koopman, Jared Leopold, Jim & Courtney Nantz, Morgan Norman, Gary van Ostrand, Michelle Ponto, Jen Pybus, Nicolas Ronteix, Keith Schaufler, Jen Scott, Lauren Scriven, Matt Valine, and Leslie Walters.

Thank you to everyone at Deutsch Family Wine & Spirits. You are too many to list, but I am grateful for your support, friendship, and passion for wine.

To my many families across the country: las amigas de Jackson, the Federal Hill troublemakers, my Georgetown friends, a summer in Portland, and the San Francisco "family."

A special thanks to Brandon McCardle and Carole Sargent for helping me bring this to life.

A special thanks also to my talented editors, Amanda Rooker and Angie Kiesling, and the fantastic crew at Morgan James Publishing.

ABOUT THE AUTHOR

Jeffrey Schiller started his career at Procter & Gamble working on global billion-dollar brands, Pringles and Cover Girl, before obtaining his MBA at Georgetown University's McDonough School of Business. He started his career in wine in 2007, as a consultant for The Four Graces winery in Oregon's Willamette Valley and later joined Treasury Wine Estates working on iconic global wine brands Wolf Blass and Beringer. In 2011, he joined wine importer Deutsch Family Wine & Spirits, where he leads the marketing efforts on one of the most popular new brands in the wine business, Josh Cellars. He is a candidate for the Wine & Spirits Education Trust Diploma and currently lives in a tiny New York City apartment. In his rare free time, he seems only to cook, eat, and drink with friends and family. He needs to go to the gym more, but instead you will find him at Smorgasbourg, Eataly, Terroir, and the Natural Science and History Museum.

FURTHER RESOURCES

Chapter 2 Shopping List

Wine

Apothic Red (California)

Barone Fini Pinot Grigio (Valdadige, Italy)

Francis Ford Coppola Diamond Collection Claret (California)

Kendall Jackson Vintner's Reserve Chardonnay (California)

Kendall Jackson Vintner's Reserve Sauvignon Blanc
(California)

Mirassou Pinot Noir (California)

Pacific Rim Dry Riesling (Columbia Valley, Washington)

Pacific Rim Sweet Riesling (Columbia Valley, Washington)

Penfolds Thomas Hyland Shiraz (Adelaide, Australia)

Robert Mondavi Private Selection Cabernet Sauvignon
(California)

Ruffino Chianti Classico (Chianti, Italy)

Santa Margherita Pinot Grigio (Alto Adige, Italy)

Food

Skim milk

Whole milk

Your preferred coffee or tea

Some sweet fruit like watermelon, kiwi, or strawberries

Olive oil, vinegar, salad greens

Chapter 4 Shopping List

Wine

Any dry white wine that is not aged in oak: this will generally
include California or New Zealand Sauvignon Blanc and
Italian Pinot Grigio. My favorites at or around $15: The
Crossings Sauvignon Blanc, Josh Cellars Sauvignon Blanc,
Kunde Sauvignon Blanc, and Barone Fini Pinot Grigio.

Any dry red wine aged in oak: this is practically every red wine
in California and around the world. My favorites at or
around $15: Josh Cellars Cabernet Sauvignon, Ruta 22
Malbec, and Kunde Zinfandel or Cabernet Sauvignon.

Any sweet white wine: [yellow tail] Moscato or Riesling are
  great.

Food

Strawberries (or a sweet red apple, kiwi, watermelon, or any
  sweet fruit)

Vinaigrette salad dressing (or olive oil and vinegar, or just a
  lemon or lime)

Lettuce or a simple, undressed salad mix

Jalapeno (or black pepper, pepperoni, hot sauce or any spicy
  pepper)

Potato chips (or pretzels, French fries, salted peanuts, or
  tortilla chips)

Grapefruit

9 781630 476311